Grade 4

Reading & Math Practice

200 Teacher-Approved Practice Pages to Build Essential Skills

New York • Toronto • London • Auckland • Sydney
Mexico City • New Delhi • Hong Kong • Buenos Aires

Teaching *Resources*

Contents

Cover design: Scott Davis
Interior design: Adrienne Downey, Melinda Belter, and Sydney Wright
Interior illustrations: Teresa Anderko, Maxie Chambliss, Steve Cox, Rusty Fletcher, Mike Gordon,
James Graham Hale, and Sydney Wright © Scholastic Inc.

"Swift Things Are Beautiful" is used by permission of the Marsh Agency Ltd.
on behalf of the Estate of Elizabeth Coatsworth.

Image credits: page 20 © Stapleton Collection/Corbis Images; page 32 © Pacific Stock-Design Pics/Superstock, Inc.;
page 52 (top) © Oktay Ortakcioglu/iStockphoto, (bottom) © mawear/iStockphoto; page 80 © Alison Wright/Corbis
Images; page 92 © Devonyu/iStockphoto; page 104 © MisterClips/iStockphoto; page 112 © Bettmann/Corbis Images;
page 128 © Paul A. Souders/Corbis Images; page 176 © Photosindia.com/Superstock, Inc.

ISBN: 978-0-545-67260-3
Written by Marcia Miller and Martin Lee.
Copyright © 2014 by Scholastic Inc.
All rights reserved. Printed in the U.S.A.
Published by Scholastic Inc.

1 2 3 4 5 6 7 8 9 10   14   21 20 19 18 17 16 15 14

Introduction

Welcome!

Reading & Math Practice: Grade 4 is the perfect way to support the learning your child needs to soar in school and beyond. The colorful, fun, and engaging activity pages in this book will give your child plenty of opportunities to practice the important reading and math skills fourth graders are expected to master. These teacher-approved practice pages are a great way to help your child:

- ☑ reinforce key academic skills and concepts
- ☑ meet curriculum standards
- ☑ prepare for standardized tests
- ☑ succeed in school
- ☑ become a lifelong learner!

Research shows that independent practice helps children gain mastery of essential skills. Each set of practice pages contains a collection of activities designed to review and reinforce a range of skills and concepts. The consistent format will help your child work independently and with confidence. Skills include:

Reading & Language Arts	Math
Word Study	Place Value
Vocabulary	Multiplication & Division
Grammar	Fractions & Decimals
Reading Comprehension	Logic & Critical Thinking
Spelling	Solving Word Problems
	Interpreting Charts & Graphs

Turn the page for information about how these exercises will help your child meet the College and Career Readiness Standards for reading, language, and mathematics. Page 5 offers suggestions for introducing the practice pages to your child along with helpful tips for making the experience go smoothly. Pages 6–9 provide a close-up look at the features in each set of practice pages.

We hope you enjoy doing the activities in this book with your child. Your involvement will help make this a valuable educational experience and will support and enhance your child's learning!

Connections to the College and Career Readiness Standards

The standards for College and Career Readiness (CCR) serve as the backbone for the practice pages in this book. These broad standards were developed to establish educational expectations meant to provide students nationwide with a quality education that prepares them for college and careers. The following lists show how the activities in this book align with the standards in key areas of focus for students in grade 4.

Standards for English Language Arts
Reading Standards (Literary and Informational Texts)
• Key Ideas and Details
• Craft and Structure
• Integration of Knowledge and Ideas
• Range of Reading Level and Text Complexity
Foundational Skills
• Phonics and Word Recognition
• Fluency
Language
• Conventions of Standard English
• Knowledge of Language
• Vocabulary Acquisition and Use

Standards for Mathematics
Mathematical Practice
1. Make sense of problems and persevere in solving them.
2. Reason abstractly and quantitatively.
3. Construct viable arguments and critique the reasoning of others.
4. Model with mathematics.
5. Use appropriate tools strategically.
6. Attend to precision.
7. Look for and make use of structure.
8. Look for and express regularity in repeating reasoning.
Mathematical Content
• Operations & Algebraic Thinking
• Number & Operations in Base Ten
• Number & Operations—Fractions
• Measurement & Data
• Geometry

Reading & Math Practice, Grade 4 © 2014 Scholastic Inc.

Getting Started

Each practice packet consists of two double-sided pages—one for reading followed by one for math. Introduce the packet to your child by going through the directions and walking through its features. Point out that activities in each section focus on different kinds of skills, and that the same features repeat throughout, always in the same order and position. In general, the practice pages progress in difficulty level and build on skills covered on previous pages. See pages 6–9 for more information.

Helpful Tips

★ For ease of use, gently tear out the pages your child will be working on along the perforated edges.

★ Invite your child to complete each packet over the course of a week, doing two or three exercises on a practice page each day.

★ If desired, allow your child to choose the order in which he or she will complete the exercises on the practice pages.

★ You'll find an answer key for each practice page, beginning on page 211. Review the answers together and encourage your child to share the thinking behind his or her answers.

★ Support your child's efforts and offer help when needed.

★ Display your child's work and share his or her progress with family and friends!

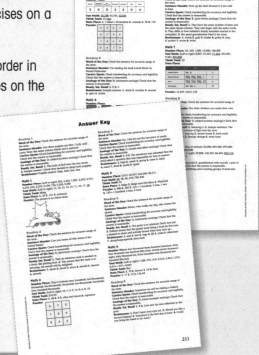

A Close-Up Look at the Practice Pages

Each of the double-sided reading practice pages includes the following skill-building features.

Reading (Side A)

Word of the Day The first feature builds vocabulary by presenting a word and its definition. A brief writing task asks your child to use the new word to demonstrate understanding of its proper usage.

Sentence Mender This feature addresses conventions of Standard English, especially spelling, capitalization, punctuation, and grammar. Your child needs to rewrite a sentence with errors correctly. A sample answer is given in the Answer Key, but your child may devise alternative corrections.

Cursive Quote This section offers your child a chance to practice cursive handwriting as he or she copies and thinks about a quotation. Your child then writes a response to a question based on the quote. For this task, direct your child to use another sheet of paper.

Analogy of the Day Every Side A concludes with an analogy that has one missing term. Your child determines the relationship between the first two words, then chooses a word to create a second pair of words that relate in the same way. He or she also writes a description of the relationship. These activities present a range of at least a dozen different types of analogies.

Reading Side A

WORD of the Day

Use the word below in a sentence about a person who explored the unknown for the first time.

pioneer: (n.) *someone who goes first, explores the unknown, or leads the way so that others can follow*

_____

_____

Sentence Mender

Rewrite the sentence to make it correct.

Bruno which walks my dog also waters the plants

_____

Cursive Quote

Copy the quotation in cursive writing.

Fall seven times, stand up eight.

—Japanese proverb

What does this proverb mean? Explain your idea in cursive on another sheet of paper.

Analogy of the Day

Complete the analogy.

Up is to **down** as _____ is to **fiction.**

○ A. fact   ○ B. book   ○ C. story   ○ D. figure

Explain how the analogy works: _____

_____

Reading & Math Practice, Grade 4 © 2014 Scholastic Inc.

Reading (Side B)

Ready, Set, Read! Side B begins with a brief fiction or nonfiction reading passage, followed by text-based questions. Tell your child to read the passage first and then answer the questions. Demonstrate how to fill in the circles for multiple-choice questions. For questions that require writing, provide an additional sheet of paper, if needed.

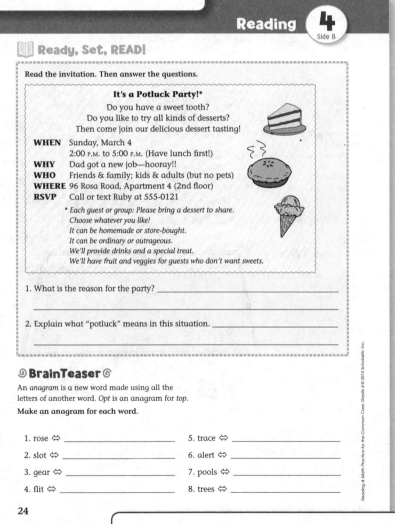

Reading 4
Side B

📖 Ready, Set, READ!

Read the invitation. Then answer the questions.

It's a Potluck Party!*

Do you have a sweet tooth?
Do you like to try all kinds of desserts?
Then come join our delicious dessert tasting!

WHEN   Sunday, March 4
2:00 P.M. to 5:00 P.M. (Have lunch first!)
WHY   Dad got a new job—hooray!!
WHO   Friends & family; kids & adults (but no pets)
WHERE 96 Rosa Road, Apartment 4 (2nd floor)
RSVP   Call or text Ruby at 555-0121

* Each guest or group: Please bring a dessert to share.
Choose whatever you like!
It can be homemade or store-bought.
It can be ordinary or outrageous.
We'll provide drinks and a special treat.
We'll have fruit and veggies for guests who don't want sweets.

1. What is the reason for the party? _____

_____

2. Explain what "potluck" means in this situation. _____

🌀 BrainTeaser 🌀

An *anagram* is a new word made using all the letters of another word. *Opt* is an anagram for *top*.

Make an anagram for each word.

1. rose ⇔ _____
2. slot ⇔ _____
3. gear ⇔ _____
4. flit ⇔ _____
5. trace ⇔ _____
6. alert ⇔ _____
7. pools ⇔ _____
8. trees ⇔ _____

24

Brainteaser Side B concludes with an entertaining word or language challenge: a puzzle, code, riddle, or other engaging task designed to stretch the mind. Encourage your child to tease out tricky solutions.

Math (Side A)

Number Place The first feature on Side A reviews place-value skills related to whole numbers, decimals, fractions, and integers. A solid place-value foundation is essential for success with computation and estimation, and for an overall grasp of numerical patterns and relationships.

Math **2**
Side A

Number Place

Write the place value of the underlined digit.

4,5_6_7 _____   12,2_8_0 _____

9,_3_56 _____   _9_3,518 _____

_4_4,212 _____   82,_6_94 _____

_1_,849 _____   7,4_6_1 _____

21_2_,873 _____   101,60_5_ _____

FAST Math

Subtract. Circle any answer that is your age.

14 – 4 = _____   16 – 9 = _____   18 – 9 = _____

17 – 8 = _____   18 – 5 = _____   15 – 7 = _____

12 – 6 = _____   18 – 10 = _____   17 – 7 = _____

Fast Math This activity addresses computation skills with the goal of building automaticity, fluency, and accuracy.

☻ Think Tank

Jin has $20. She bought flowers for $3.50 and a gift for $2 more than that. She bought a card for $1.95. How much did she spend in all?

_____

Show your work in the tank.

17

Think Tank This feature offers a word problem that draws from a wide spectrum of grade-appropriate skills, strategies, and approaches. In the think tank itself, your child can draw, do computations, and work out his or her thinking.

Math (Side B)

> **Data Place** In this section, your child solves problems based on reading, collecting, representing, and interpreting data that is presented in many formats: lists, tables, charts, pictures, and, especially, graphs.

Data Place

Use the circle graph about singers in the high school chorus to answer the questions.

High School Chorus

Basses 8 · Sopranos 16 · Altos 12 · Tenors 12

1. How many singers are in the chorus? _____

2. How many basses are in the chorus? _____

3. Which sections of the chorus have the same number of members?

   _____

4. Which section has twice the number of members as the bass section does?

   _____

Puzzler

A magic square is an ancient math puzzle. The Chinese first made the puzzle over 2,600 years ago.

The numbers from 1–9 appear only *once* each in the 9 boxes of the square. The sum of each row, column, and diagonal must be 15. Three of the numbers are already in place. Figure out which numbers go in the other boxes.

Explain your solution method.

6		
	5	
8		

_____

_____

> **Puzzler** Side B always ends with some form of an entertaining challenge: a brainteaser, puzzle, code, or other engaging task designed to stretch the mind.

Use the word below in a sentence about a daily habit that helps you get ready for school.

routine: (n.) *a regular or usual way to do things; habit*

_____

_____

Sentence Mender

Rewrite the sentence to make it correct.

Are 3 puppys our Moe Curly and Larry

_____

Cursive Quote

Copy the quotation in cursive writing.

Every path has its puddle.

—Anonymous

_____

_____

_____

Do you agree with this proverb? Write your answer in cursive on another sheet of paper.

Analogy of the Day

Complete the analogy.

Flower is to **garden** as _____ is to **playground**.

○ A. desk   ○ B. school   ○ C. park   ○ D. slide

Explain how the analogy works: _____

_____

📖 Ready, Set, READ!

Read the story. Then answer the questions.

Picking a Pup

Mom and I were so excited as we arrived at the animal shelter. We couldn't wait to pick our new puppy. An employee soon approached us carrying a tiny ball of fluff under each arm. She smiled and led us into a tiny room. She left us there with both pups and said, "They're sisters. Take all the time you need." She closed the door and left us with two adorable mutts. How would we ever decide? They looked like twins.

One scampered right over and jumped on us. She chewed on my sneaker laces and licked my face. Mom and I were smiling our heads off. While this frisky pup was nibbling on my fingers, her sister was moving slowly around the edges of the room. She sniffed at each corner. Next she came to sniff us, too. Then she sat by our feet, looked up at us, and rolled onto her back for a tummy rub.

We made our choice.

1. What were the "tiny balls of fluff" the employee carried?

   _____

   _____

2. What choice do you think they made? Explain.

   _____

   _____

🌀 BrainTeaser 🌀

Climb the word ladder to change *lamp* to *fire*. Change only one letter at a time. Write the new word on each step.

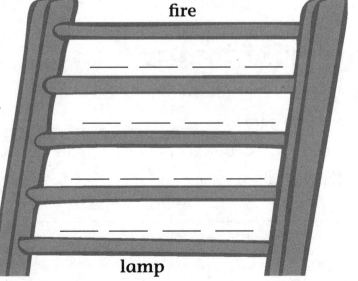

fire

lamp

Reading & Math Practice, Grade 4 © 2014 Scholastic Inc.

Number Place

Write the number that is 100 *more*.

202 _____   3,155 _____   7,187 _____

2,103 _____   2,661 _____   9,119 _____

Write the number that is 100 *less*.

323 _____   2,379 _____   2,296 _____

834 _____   5,405 _____   5,140 _____

FAST Math

Add. Circle the greatest sum.

4 + 7 = _____   9 + 6 = _____   8 + 7 = _____

3 + 9 = _____   6 + 9 = _____   8 + 3 = _____

7 + 9 = _____   8 + 9 = _____   9 + 9 = _____

Think Tank

Ken has fewer absences than Meg, but more than Dan. Ming has been absent more than Meg. Who has been absent the most?

_____

Show your work in the tank.

Reading & Math Practice, Grade 4 © 2014 Scholastic Inc.

Data Place

The table shows some different sports equipment sold at a sporting goods store one week.

Use the data in the table to answer the questions.

Item	Number Sold
Baseball Glove	19
Soccer Ball	31
Tennis Racquet	17
Hockey Stick	24
Swimsuit	60

1. How many hockey sticks were sold? _____

2. How many of the sports items were sold in all? _____

3. Which item sold about three times as much as the baseball glove did?

_____

Puzzler

Count *on* by 11 to connect the dots.

Hint: There are six numbers not used.

What picture did you make?

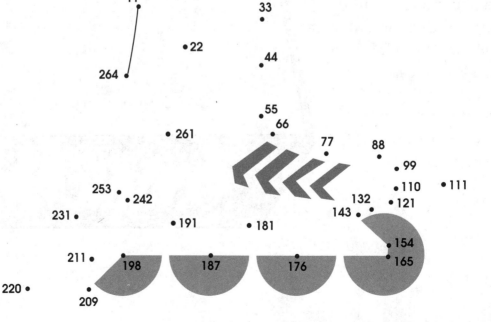

14

WORD of the Day

Use the word below in a sentence about the basic goal of a sport or game you enjoy.

basic: (adj.) *main part; at the root of; underlying; primary*

_____

_____

Sentence Mender

Rewrite the sentence to make it correct.

can you name all fivety States of the united states

_____

Cursive Quote

Copy the quotation in cursive writing.

A half truth is a whole lie.

—Jewish proverb

_____

_____

_____

_____

What does this saying mean? Write your answer in cursive on another sheet of paper.

Analogy of the Day

Complete the analogy.

Flat is to **level** as _____ is to **large**.

○ A. small   ○ B. big   ○ C. straight   ○ D. tiny

Explain how the analogy works: _____

_____

📖 Ready, Set, READ!

Read the e-mail. Then answer the questions.

Hey Trey,

My dad is taking Katy and me apple picking on Saturday. He says you can come, too, if it's okay with your mom. The apple orchard is less than an hour away, past a waterfall and a llama ranch. Dad loves fresh apples (and I love apple pie!), so he needs some willing farmhands!

Apple picking isn't hard work. In fact, it's pretty fun. I've done it before, so I know. Plus it's active, tasty, AND can be quite messy! Oh, did I mention the bonus? On the way back, we usually stop at this great ice-cream stand. They have maybe ten flavors, but each one is so creamy, your mouth will faint!

Please let me know by tomorrow, if you can. If you can't come, I'll invite another friend. But you're my first choice, pal.

Randy

1. What do farmhands do?

_____

_____

2. What does Randy mean by telling Trey that his *mouth will faint*?

_____

_____

🌀 BrainTeaser 🌀

Use the clues to complete a word that starts with *sho*.

1. Footwear   S H O ___ ___

2. Rattled   S H O ___ ___

3. Coastline   S H O ___ ___

4. Ought to   S H O ___ ___ ___

5. Place to wash off   S H O ___ ___ ___

6. Tools for digging   S H O ___ ___ ___ ___

16

Number Place

Write the place value of the underlined digit.

4,5_6_7 _____   1_2_,280 _____

9,_3_56 _____   _9_3,518 _____

_4_4,212 _____   82,_6_94 _____

_1_,849 _____   7,4_6_1 _____

2_1_2,873 _____   _1_01,605 _____

FAST Math ➡

Subtract. Circle any answer that is your age.

14 – 4 = _____   16 – 9 = _____   18 – 9 = _____

17 – 8 = _____   18 – 5 = _____   15 – 7 = _____

12 – 6 = _____   18 – 10 = _____   17 – 7 = _____

💡 Think Tank

Jin has $20. She bought flowers for $3.50 and a gift for $2 more than that. She bought a card for $1.95. How much did she spend in all?

_____

Show your work in the tank.

Data Place

Use the circle graph about singers in the high school chorus to answer the questions.

High School Chorus

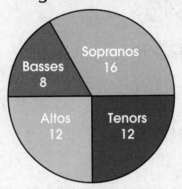

1. How many singers are in the chorus? _____

2. How many basses are in the chorus? _____

3. Which sections of the chorus have the same number of members?

   _____

4. Which section has twice the number of members as the bass section does?

   _____

Puzzler

A magic square is an ancient math puzzle. The Chinese first made the puzzle over 2,600 years ago.

The numbers from 1–9 appear only *once* each in the 9 boxes of the square. The sum of each row, column, and diagonal must be 15. Three of the numbers are already in place. Figure out which numbers go in the other boxes.

Explain your solution method.

6		
	5	
8		

_____

_____

Reading & Math Practice, Grade 4 © 2014 Scholastic Inc.

WORD of the Day

Use the word below in a sentence to describe something you recite or sing in this way.

chant: (v.) *to sing or say over and over again in rhythm*

_____

_____

Sentence Mender

Rewrite the sentence to make it correct.

No I did not eet the last peace of candie

_____

Cursive Quote

Copy the quotation in cursive writing.

Never, never, never give up.

—Sir Winston Churchill

_____
_____
_____
_____

Explain why Churchill's advice could be hard to follow. Write your explanation in cursive on another sheet of paper.

Analogy of the Day

Complete the analogy.

Hungry is to **eat** as _____ is to **cry**.

O A. yell   O B. happy   O C. sad   O D. tears

Explain how the analogy works: _____

_____

19

📖 Ready, Set, READ!

Read the folktale. Then answer the questions.

Shield and Spear   *A Chinese Folktale*

A merchant brought his shields and spears to market. He hung a banner to attract buyers. Soon onlookers gathered. The merchant held a shield above his head. He boasted, "Behold my shield! See its bold design! Notice its excellent quality, its perfect shape! No spear on earth can pierce it! My shield gives the safest protection! Buy one to become a respected warrior!"

The merchant put down the shield and picked up a spear. He raised it high above his head. He shouted, "Behold my spear of death! It is the sharpest spear on earth. My mighty spear can pierce any shield, no matter how hard, in one blow! Buy one to become a champion in battle!"

The merchant put down his spear, pleased with his speeches. A child came forward, saying, "Excuse me, sir. If I use your sharpest spear to strike your strongest shield, what will happen then?"

The merchant gulped. He opened his mouth but could find no answer. He rolled up his banner and left the market.

1. What is the job of a merchant?

   ○ A. joking   ○ B. selling   ○ C. fighting   ○ D. protecting

2. Why did the merchant suddenly leave?

   _____

   _____

🌀 BrainTeaser 🌀

Each word below is missing the same letter from its beginning and end. Complete every word using a *different* missing letter pair.

1. ____ ig ____

2. ____ omi ____

3. ____ oin ____

4. ____ ras ____

5. ____ abe ____

6. ____ azo ____

7. ____ rie ____

8. ____ earl ____

9. ____ ypis ____

Reading & Math Practice, Grade 4 © 2014 Scholastic Inc.

Number Place

Write each number in standard form.

three thousand fifteen _____

twenty-nine thousand four hundred thirty-seven _____

six hundred forty-three thousand _____

eighty-two thousand three hundred eleven _____

FAST Math

Add. Circle any answer that is an odd number.

17 + 48	29 + 29	38 + 58	125 + 345	134 + 656	417 + 417

Think Tank

Lisa has a package that costs $3.95 to mail. She pays with 3 dollar bills and 4 quarters. How much change should Lisa get back?

_____

Show your work in the tank.

Data Place

Use the graph about trail lengths to answer the questions.

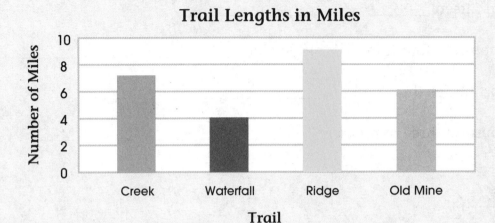

Trail Lengths in Miles

1. Which is the longest trail? _____

2. Which two trails have a combined length of 15 miles? _____

_____

3. Which trail is 5 miles shorter than the Ridge Trail? _____

Puzzler

A dart can earn three different values.

• A dart in the center earns 100.
• A dart in the white ring earns 10.
• A dart in the outer ring earns 2.

Try these challenges:

1. What is the best score you can get with

   8 darts? _____

2. What would you earn with 5 darts in each

   section? _____

3. Draw 5 red darts to make a score of 132.

4. Draw 10 blue darts to make a score of 150.

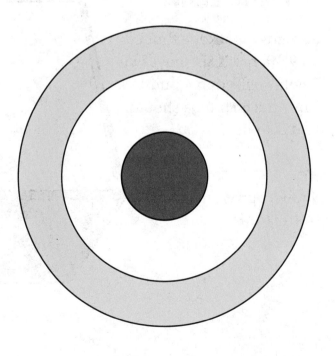

Reading & Math Practice, Grade 4 © 2014 Scholastic Inc.

WORD of the Day

Use the word below in a sentence about a person who explored the unknown for the first time.

pioneer: (n.) *someone who goes first, explores the unknown, or leads the way so that others can follow*

_____

_____

Sentence Mender

Rewrite the sentence to make it correct.

Bruno which walks my dog also waters the plants

_____

Cursive Quote

Copy the quotation in cursive writing.

Fall seven times, stand up eight.

—Japanese proverb

_____

_____

_____

What does this proverb mean? Explain your idea in cursive on another sheet of paper.

Analogy of the Day

Complete the analogy.

Up is to **down** as _____ is to **fiction**.

○ A. fact   ○ B. book   ○ C. story   ○ D. figure

Explain how the analogy works: _____

_____

📖 Ready, Set, READ!

Read the invitation. Then answer the questions.

It's a Potluck Party!*

Do you have a sweet tooth?
Do you like to try all kinds of desserts?
Then come join our delicious dessert tasting!

WHEN   Sunday, March 4
2:00 P.M. to 5:00 P.M. (Have lunch first!)
WHY   Dad got a new job—hooray!!
WHO   Friends & family; kids & adults (but no pets)
WHERE 96 Rosa Road, Apartment 4 (2nd floor)
RSVP   Call or text Ruby at 555-0121

* Each guest or group: Please bring a dessert to share.
Choose whatever you like!
It can be homemade or store-bought.
It can be ordinary or outrageous.
We'll provide drinks and a special treat.
We'll have fruit and veggies for guests who don't want sweets.

1. What is the reason for the party? _____

_____

2. Explain what "potluck" means in this situation. _____

_____

🌀 BrainTeaser 🌀

An *anagram* is a new word made using all the
letters of another word. *Opt* is an anagram for *top*.

Make an anagram for each word.

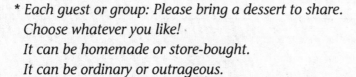

1. rose ⇔ _____

2. slot ⇔ _____

3. gear ⇔ _____

4. flit ⇔ _____

5. trace ⇔ _____

6. alert ⇔ _____

7. pools ⇔ _____

8. trees ⇔ _____

Number Place

Write each number in word form.

4,319 _____

44,159 _____

27,008 _____

60,006 _____

309,254 _____

FAST Math

Add. Find the sum of the greatest and least answers.

3,016 + 4,410 = _____   140 + 807 = _____   249 + 370 = _____

1,209 + 7,005 = _____   4,254 + 1,709 = _____   156 + 918 = _____

_____ + _____ = _____

Think Tank

Alex, Ben, Cindy, and Dee are in line for a movie. Alex is third in line. Dee is ahead of Cindy, but behind Ben. Who is first in line?

_____

Show your work in the tank.

Reading & Math Practice, Grade 4 © 2014 Scholastic Inc.

Data Place

Greenleaf School voted on a school mascot.

Use the graph to answer the questions.

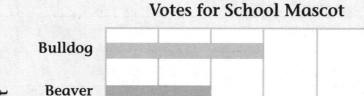
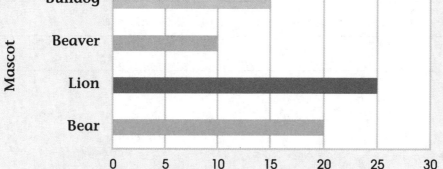

Votes for School Mascot

1. How many people voted in the survey? _____

2. Which mascot got the fewest votes? _____

3. How many more kids voted for Lion than for Bulldog? _____

4. Suppose 10 more kids voted and gave Bear 8 votes and Lion 2 votes.

   Which animal would be the mascot? _____

Puzzler

Use the number
with each pet to
solve the number
sentences below.

3	5	8	10	2	7

1. + = _____

3. ÷ ⬭ = _____

2. ×  = _____

4. × = _____

26

Reading & Math Practice, Grade 4 © 2014 Scholastic Inc.

WORD of the Day

Use the word below in a sentence to describe a rough object.

coarse: (adj.) *rough in texture; harsh to the touch*

_____

_____

Sentence Mender

Rewrite the sentence to make it correct.

Tomorro we will be vizit a bakery

_____

Cursive Quote

Copy the quotation in cursive writing.

Try and fail, but don't fail to try.

—Stephen Kaggwa

- -

- -

- -

- -

What does Kaggwa mean by this saying? Write your answer in cursive on another sheet of paper.

Analogy of the Day

Complete the analogy.

Number is to **eight** as _____ is to **sandwich**.

○ A. sixteen   ○ B. ate   ○ C. eat   ○ D. food

Explain how the analogy works: _____

_____

Ready, Set, READ!

Read the fable. Then answer the questions.

Lion and Rabbit   *An Indian Fable From the Panchatantra*

Long ago, Lion ruled the jungle. He was vain and greedy. The other animals lived in fear. They decided that one animal per kind would offer itself to Lion every day. They hoped this would calm Lion so the others might live in peace. So the plan began.

Soon a rabbit had to offer itself. The oldest, wisest rabbit came forward. She went quietly to meet her fate. When Rabbit reached Lion, he was both hungry and annoyed.

Rabbit spoke softly. "Master, my kind walked me here. But another lion attacked us by surprise. He killed the other rabbits. I managed to escape with my life, which I now offer to you," she said. "But I think that other lion may challenge you."

Lion growled in rage. "Show me this challenger!" he demanded. So Rabbit led Lion to a deep pool. She pointed to the "other" lion in the water. Lion roared and bared his fangs at that beast, who responded with equal anger. Lion dove into the pool to attack his rival, but drowned.

MORAL: Intelligence can defeat might.

1. Which word means the same as *vain*?

   ○ A. strong   ○ B. proud   ○ C. lazy   ○ D. humble

2. What did Lion really see? _____

   _____

๑ BrainTeaser ๑

The words in each group make a sentence, but only if you put them in order. Start each sentence with a capital letter. Use an end mark.

1. yet eyes don't your open

   _____

2. would a second like you helping

   _____

3. of is June day first tomorrow the

   _____

4. the salad table could to bring the you

   _____

Reading & Math Practice, Grade 4 © 2014 Scholastic Inc.

Number Place

Label the columns on the place value chart below from *Ones* to *Millions*.

Record the number that has *2 thousands, 8 hundreds, 5 ten-thousands, 0 hundred-thousands, 4 ones, 3 millions, and 0 tens.*

FAST Math

Add. Circle any answer that is an even number.

```
   1,712          34,128            314
     421           2,218         31,004
 + 8,065         + 5,835             52
                                +   666
```

Think Tank

A scientist found 84 dinosaur eggs in one location and 201 in another location. She had expected to find 300 eggs. By how much did she miss her goal?

_____

Show your work in the tank.

Data Place

Fourth graders took a survey about favorite kinds of movies.

Use the graph to answer the questions.

Movies We Like Best

Horror	🎟️ 🎟️ 🎟️
Adventure	🎟️ 🎟️
Comedy	🎟️ 🎟️
Fantasy	🎟️ 🎟️ 🎟️ 🎟️ 🎟️
Animated	🎟️ 🎟️ 🎟️ 🎟️ 🎟️ 🎟️

Key 🎟️ = 10 students

1. What does the key show? _____

2. Which kind of movie do 15 students like best? _____

3. Animated films got _____ more votes than horror films.

4. How many students were surveyed? _____

Puzzler

Solve the number puzzle. Use only the numbers 5, 6, 7, and 8 *once* inside every small square, and *once* in every row and column.

		8	
8	7		6
		6	5
5	6		

Use the word below in a sentence about something you helped to grow or expand.

increase: (v.) *to make or become larger in size or greater in number; to add to; to make grow, swell, or expand*

_____

_____

Sentence Mender

Rewrite the sentence to make it correct.

Im reading the book lizzerd music by daniel pinkwater

_____

Cursive Quote

Copy the quotation in cursive writing.

A chattering bird builds no nest.

—African proverb

- -

- -

_____

Explain what you think this proverb means. Write your answer in cursive on another sheet of paper.

Analogy of the Day

Complete the analogy.

He is to **she** as _____ is to **here**.

○ A. him   ○ B. there   ○ C. they   ○ D. their

Explain how the analogy works: _____

_____

📖 Ready, Set, READ!

Read the passage. Then answer the questions.

The UN-Fish

Tube feet

The creature most people call a starfish is misnamed. Its official scientific name is the sea star. Let's discover how sea stars differ from actual fish.

• Fish are vertebrates; they have backbones. Sea stars are invertebrates because they have no backbone. Their nearest relatives are other invertebrates: sea urchins, sea cucumbers, and sand dollars.

• Fish swim but can't walk. Sea stars walk but can't swim. Sea stars crawl on tiny tube feet, which grow on the underside of each arm. Tube feet end in stretchy suckers.

• Fish get oxygen as water moves through their gills. Sea stars get oxygen from the water their tube feet suck in!

• Fish have one stomach; sea stars have two. One stomach always stays in the body to digest food. The other acts as a traveling mouth. It comes out of the sea star's body to wrap around food the sea star traps with its tube feet. It takes that food back to the inside stomach for digesting.

1. Why is a sea star *not* a fish?
   ○ A. It is too slow.
   ○ B. It has tube feet.
   ○ C. It needs oxygen.
   ○ D. It has no backbone.

2. Which is *not* a job of tube feet?
   ○ A. sucking
   ○ B. crawling
   ○ C. digesting
   ○ D. trapping

🌀 BrainTeaser 🌀

Onomatopoeia is a word that sounds like what it means. Examples are *buzz*, *hiss*, and *oink*.

Finish each simple sentence with onomatopoeia.

1. Soda cans _____ .

2. A wood fire _____ .

3. Leaves _____ .

4. Water balloons _____ .

5. Heavy chains _____ .

32

Reading & Math Practice, Grade 4 © 2014 Scholastic Inc.

Number Place

Rewrite each number as only hundreds, only tens, or only ones.

Number	equals	Hundreds	or	Tens	or	Ones
300		3		30		300
600				60		
1,800						1,800
2,700		27				

FAST Math

Add. Circle the sum closest to 500,000.

43,000 + 195,000 = _____

56,000 + 48,000 = _____

260,000 + 250,000 = _____

22,000 + 7,000 = _____

37,000 + 540,000 = _____

880,000 + 55,000 = _____

Think Tank

Use the menu. Juan orders 3 burritos, 2 burgers, 4 sodas, and 1 juice. He pays with a $20 bill. What is his change?

_____

Show your work in the tank.

MENU

Burrito $2.19
Burger $1.79
Corn Dog . . . $1.33
Egg Roll. $1.49
Juice $1.09
Soda $1.20
Tea . . . . $ .55
Milk . . . . $ .60

Think Tank

Data Place

A clothing store is taking a T-shirt inventory.

Complete the table to show all of the results.

T-Shirt Inventory

T-Shirt	Sizes			Total
	S	M	L	
Short Sleeve	27	35	42	
Long Sleeve	36		21	75
V-Neck	49	9	31	89
Turtleneck	37	22		86
Sports Jersey		5	12	26

Puzzler

The shape below uses 5 squares and has a perimeter of 12 units.

Draw a shape that also uses 5 squares but has a perimeter of 10 units.

WORD of the Day

Use the word below in a sentence predicting something you might be doing ten years from now.

decade: (n.) *a period of ten years*

_____

_____

Sentence Mender

Rewrite the sentence to make it correct.

Turn up the heat cuz it is to cold in hear

_____

Cursive Quote

Copy the quotation in cursive writing.

Whatever you are, be a good one.

—Abraham Lincoln

- - - - - - - - - - - - - - - - - - - -

_____

- - - - - - - - - - - - - - - - - - - -

_____

How can any person make this goal come true? Write your answer in cursive on another sheet of paper.

Analogy of the Day

Complete the analogy.

Toe is to **foot** as _____ is to **face**.

○ A. finger   ○ B. nose   ○ C. head   ○ D. knee

Explain how the analogy works: _____

_____

📖 Ready, Set, READ!

Read the poem.
Then answer the questions.

Caterpillar

Little Isabella Miller
Had a fuzzy caterpillar.
First it crawled upon her mother,
Then upon her baby brother.
They said, "Isabella Miller!
Put away your caterpillar!"

Little Isabella Miller
Had a fuzzy caterpillar.
First it crawled upon her brother,
Then upon her great-grandmother.
Gran said, "Isabella Miller,
How I love your caterpillar!"

1. How are the two verses alike?

_____
_____
_____
_____
_____

2. How do the two verses differ?

_____
_____
_____
_____
_____

3. Which person in Isabella's family liked her caterpillar most? _____
_____

🌀 BrainTeaser 🌀

Complete each saying below using a word from the word bank.

1. Actions speak louder than _____ .

2. All that glitters is not _____ .

3. Don't put all your eggs in one _____ .

4. Honesty is the best _____ .

5. Look before you _____ .

6. Practice makes _____ .

7. The early bird gets the _____ .

8. You can't teach an old dog new _____ .

Word Bank

gold
leap
tricks
worm
words
policy
basket
perfect

36

Number Place

Write how many are in one million.

hundred-thousands in one million _____

ten-thousands in one million _____

thousands in one million _____

hundreds in one million _____

tens in one million _____

FAST Math

Add. Circle any answer that is an even number.

1,742 + 7,065	35,128 + 58,235	60,128 + 11,234
305,549 + 188,032	3,122 + 6,239	239,127 + 452,731

Think Tank

Lin found 17 Web sites that have photos of Venus. José found 4 of those sites and 5 others that Lin did not find. How many different Web sites did they find in all?

_____

Show you work
in the tank.

Data Place

The table below shows results of a survey on favorite kinds of sandwiches. Some of the table is blank.

Use the clues to complete the table.

- Twelve people chose hamburger.

- Tuna got the most votes.

- Twice as many people like grilled cheese better than peanut butter.

Sandwich	Tally	Number
	ⅢⅠ Ⅲ	
		16
		18
	ⅢⅠ ⅢⅠ Ⅱ	

Puzzler

Use the numbers in the figure to solve the problems below.

Find the sum of numbers:

- *not* inside the oval or triangle

  _____

- both inside the triangle and the oval

  _____

- inside the triangle *only*

  _____

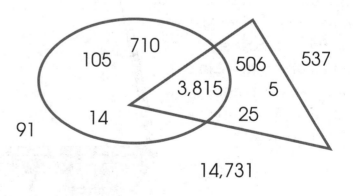

Reading & Math Practice, Grade 4 © 2014 Scholastic Inc.

WORD of the Day

Use the word below in a sentence that suggests why people fear toxic waste dumps.

toxic: (adj.) *poisonous, deadly*

_____

_____

Sentence Mender

Rewrite the sentence to make it correct.

The older childrins can make there own lunchs

_____

Cursive Quote

Copy the quotation in cursive writing.

Repetition is the mother of learning.

—White Mountain Apache saying

_____

_____

_____

Do you agree with this idea? Explain your answer in cursive on another sheet of paper.

Analogy of the Day

Complete the analogy.

Desk is to **classroom** as _____ is to **solar system**.

○ A. school   ○ B. student   ○ C. universe   ○ D. planet

Explain how the analogy works: _____

_____

Ready, Set, READ!

Read the dictionary entry.
Then answer the questions.

beam (beem)

1. noun A ray or band of light from a flashlight, a car headlight, or the sun.

2. noun A long, thick piece of wood, concrete, or metal used to support the roof or floors of a building.

3. verb To shine. *The sun beamed across the water.*

4. verb To smile widely. *Greg beamed when he saw the "A" on his report.*

***verb* beaming, beamed**

1. Which meaning of **beam** fits when you are very happy?

_____

2. Write a sentence that uses **beam** as a noun.

_____

_____

_____

_____

_____

⊚ BrainTeaser ⊚

Hink Pinks are one-syllable word pairs that rhyme to fit clues.
Solve these Hink Pink riddles.

Example

angry father = mad dad

1. What is the label on a paper sack? _____

2. Where do Mickey and Minnie live? _____

3. Where is a cozy place to read? _____

4. Who is the best collector of postage? _____

5. What are unusual coins given back? _____

6. What is a shabby trumpet? _____

40

Number Place

Write the number 1,000 *less*.

_____ 60,000

_____ 900,000

_____ 1,000,000

Write the number 1,000 *more*.

2,399 _____

54,799 _____

999,000 _____

FAST Math

Add. Circle the answer closest to one million.

```
   21,746
+   8,062
_____
```

```
   31,424
+ 88,935
_____
```

```
   67,121
+ 19,284
_____
```

```
  360,040
+ 582,072
_____
```

```
    3,122
+ 466,239
_____
```

```
  939,183
+ 462,531
_____
```

Think Tank

Pete's Pizza offers 5 toppings and 4 kinds of crust. How many *different* pizzas could be made using 1 topping and 1 kind of crust?

_____

Make a list or diagram the choices in the tank.

TOPPING	CRUST
Mushrooms	Regular
Onion	Thin
Pepperoni	Whole Wheat
Sausage	Very Thick
Extra Cheese	

Think Tank

Reading & Math Practice, Grade 4 © 2014 Scholastic Inc.

Data Place

Draw each point on the coordinate grid. Then connect the points in order to make a closed figure.

$(2, 1) \rightarrow (4, 3) \rightarrow (7, 3) \rightarrow (9, 1) \rightarrow (2, 1)$

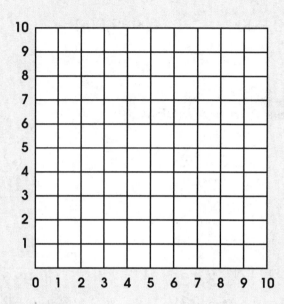

1. What figure did you make? _____

2. Describe the figure. _____

3. Name four points you can connect to make a square. _____

_____

Puzzler

How many line segments are there in this figure?

● ———————— ● ———————— ● ———————— ● ———————— ●

Explain how you counted the segments. _____

_____

Reading & Math Practice, Grade 4 © 2014 Scholastic Inc.

WORD of the Day

Use the word below in a sentence that tells about how a well-trained service dog can help someone in need.

assist: (v.) *to help or aid*

_____

_____

Sentence Mender

Rewrite the sentence to make it correct.

Jason asked can you help me find my keys

_____

Cursive Quote

Copy the quotation in cursive writing.

We read to know we are not alone.

—C.S. Lewis

_____

_____

_____

How can reading affect a person's mood? Explain in cursive on another sheet of paper.

Analogy of the Day

Complete the analogy.

Warm is to **hot** as _____ is to **cold**.

○ A. hot   ○ B. cool   ○ C. ice   ○ D. humid

Explain how the analogy works: _____

_____

📖 Ready, Set, READ!

Read the story. Then answer the questions.

Stay Near

When Scott hiked the mountains, his dog Bailey always came along. "Stay near," Scott would command, and Bailey always did. Well, almost always.

They were high on their favorite trail one day. Near dusk, Scott stopped to rest before descending. At that moment Bailey spotted a rabbit—and off he dashed. Scott shouted, "Bailey! Stay near!" He sprinted after his dog, repeating the command. He ran and shouted until he was out of breath, but Bailey was out of sight.

It was now fully dark. Scott phoned a friend to report that he would stay on the mountain all night; he would never abandon Bailey. Scott built a fire. He hollered for Bailey until his throat ached. Hours passed and still no dog. Finally, Scott fell asleep, feeling gloomy and scared. He dreamed of the beach, of surf tickling his toes. A huge wave washed over his face, waking him with a start. Bailey was licking his cheek.

1. What does *descending* mean?

   ○ A. relaxing   ○ B. daydreaming   ○ C. climbing   ○ D. going down

2. Why did Scott call a friend? _____

   _____

🌀 BrainTeaser 🌀

Hinky Pinkies are two-syllable word pairs that rhyme to fit clues.
Solve these Hinky Pinky riddles.

Example

arctic tooth = polar molar

1. What is a clever cat? _____

2. What is a box for huge rocks? _____

3. What is knitwear for a baby cat paw? _____

4. What is odder trouble? _____

5. What is a soft shaky tummy? _____

6. What is a fortunate swimming bird? _____

44

Reading & Math Practice, Grade 4 © 2014 Scholastic Inc.

Number Place

Write the number 10,000 *less*.

_____ 60,000

_____ 900,000

_____ 1,000,000

Write the number 100,000 *more*.

27,399 _____

564,799 _____

888,888 _____

FAST Math

Subtract. Circle any answer whose digits add to less than 10.

$$
\begin{array}{r} 746 \\ -\ 332 \\ \hline \end{array}
\qquad
\begin{array}{r} 88 \\ -\ 67 \\ \hline \end{array}
\qquad
\begin{array}{r} 657 \\ -\ 204 \\ \hline \end{array}
$$

$$
\begin{array}{r} 6,949 \\ -\ 5,822 \\ \hline \end{array}
\qquad
\begin{array}{r} 578 \\ -\ 466 \\ \hline \end{array}
\qquad
\begin{array}{r} 9,896 \\ -\ 4,625 \\ \hline \end{array}
$$

Think Tank

Saul's school is setting up chairs in the gym. Students have already set up 135 chairs. They will set up 320 in all. How many more chairs do they need to set up?

_____

Show your work in the tank.

Data Place

The table shows the number of players in different sports leagues.

Use the data in the table to answer the questions.

Team	Players
Baseball	625
Soccer	420
Football	666
Hockey	222
Lacrosse	105

1. How many more players are in the football league than the baseball league?

_____

2. Which league has four times as many players as the lacrosse league has?

_____

3. Which league has one-third as many players as the football league?

_____

Puzzler

Trace over the design below without lifting your pencil or retracing any lines.

Try it first with your finger.

Then use a pencil or marker.

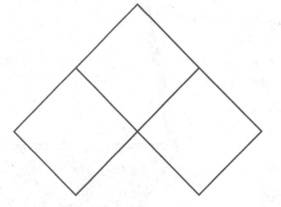

46

WORD of the Day

Use the word below in a sentence to describe something you do in a careless hurry.

haste: (n) *the act of hurrying; careless rushing*

_____

_____

Sentence Mender

Rewrite the sentence to make it correct.

The science teach gives we short quizs every days

_____

Cursive Quote

Copy the quotation in cursive writing.

Let your conscience be your guide.

—Jiminy Cricket (cartoon character)

- -

- -

- -

How does your conscience guide you? Write your answer in cursive on another sheet of paper.

Analogy of the Day

Complete the analogy.

Whimper is to **cry** as _____ is to **laugh.**

○ A. laughter   ○ B. timid   ○ C. giggle   ○ D. funny

Explain how the analogy works: _____

_____

📖 Ready, Set, READ!

Read the passage. Then answer the questions.

Geographic Center of United States

It's pretty easy to find the center of a circle. A circle is a *regular* figure. Every point around the edge is as far from the center as every other. If you put a pin in that center, the circle would balance.

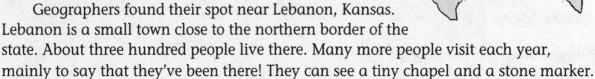

It's harder to find the center of an *irregular* figure. Picture the United States—leaving out Alaska and Hawaii. Our nation has a center. But where?

The best answer is an estimate. Geographers have made a fairly close one. They pictured the "lower 48" as one mass. Then they used advanced math. They figured out the point where this mass would balance.

Geographers found their spot near Lebanon, Kansas. Lebanon is a small town close to the northern border of the state. About three hundred people live there. Many more people visit each year, mainly to say that they've been there! They can see a tiny chapel and a stone marker.

1. What makes it harder to find the center of an irregular figure than of a regular one?

_____

_____

2. Why do you think geographers left out Alaska and Hawaii in their work?

_____

_____

🌀 BrainTeaser 🌀

Unscramble each dance word.
Write it correctly in the spaces.
Then unscramble the boxed letters
to name another dance word.

_____

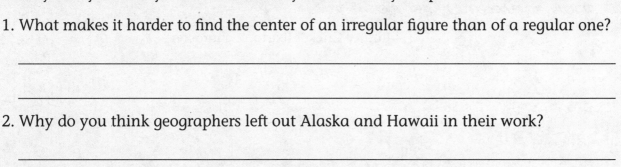

KALOP

SWITT

ANGOT

TELLBA

LOBORE

ERLE

Reading & Math Practice, Grade 4 © 2014 Scholastic Inc.

Number Place

Compare. Write **<**, **=**, or **>**.

20,999 _____ 29,000   15,551 _____ 15,155

9,988 _____ 10,000   90,404 _____ 91,777

6,678 _____ sixty-six thousand seventy-eight

forty-five thousand three hundred _____ 45,300

FAST Math

Subtract. Circle any answer whose digits add to 10.

```
   7,464        838          657
 - 3,127      - 657        - 294
```

```
   6,345       5,738       9,816
 - 5,812     - 4,266     - 7,425
```

Think Tank

It is 139 miles from Phoenix, AZ, to Flagstaff, AZ. From there it is 79 more miles to the Grand Canyon. How far is it from Phoenix to the Grand Canyon?

_____

Show your work in the tank.

Reading & Math Practice, Grade 4 © 2014 Scholastic Inc.

Data Place

Students were asked how many hours they spend each week using social media. The line plot shows the results.

Use the data in the line plot to answer the questions.

Hours Spent Using Social Media

```
                        X
                        X
            X   X   X
            X   X   X
            X   X   X
            X   X   X   X
    X   X   X   X   X   X   X
    X   X   X   X   X   X   X           X
  ─────────────────────────────────────────
    0   1   2   3   4   5   6   7   8   9   10
```

1. How many students were surveyed? _____

2. What is the range of the data? _____

3. What answer came up most often? _____

4. How many students spend 5 hours each week using social media? _____

5. How many students spend less than 5 hours each week using social media? _____

Puzzler

Use each digit from 1–9 once only to form three addends whose sum is 999.

$$
\begin{array}{r}
\square\ \square\ \square \\
\square\ \square\ \square \\
+\ \square\ \square\ \square \\
\hline
\end{array}
$$

50

WORD of the Day

Use the word below in a sentence about a mountain range.

jagged: (adj.) *having a ragged or uneven edge with many sharp high points and deep notches*

_____

_____

Sentence Mender

Rewrite the sentence to make it correct.

How many legs does spiders has

_____

Cursive Quote

Copy the quotation in cursive writing.

If you can read this, thank a teacher.

—Anonymous

_____

_____

_____

How does reading help you in your life? Explain in cursive on another sheet of paper.

Analogy of the Day

Complete the analogy.

Rooster is to **crow** as _____ is to **neigh**.

○ A. horse   ○ B. chicken   ○ C. purr   ○ D. agree

Explain how the analogy works: _____

_____

📖 Ready, Set, READ!

Read the passage. Then answer the questions.

Why Opossum Has a Bare Tail   *A Creek/Muscogee Tale of Tails*

One night, Opossum spied his friend Raccoon. Opossum had always loved Raccoon's bushy tail with many rings. So Opossum asked, "Raccoon, how did you get those rings?"

Raccoon proudly stroked his tail and answered, "I created them myself. First I wrapped strips of bark around my tail here and here and here," he pointed. "Then I held my tail over a fire. The uncovered fur turned black. But the fur under the bark stayed light, as you see. Lovely, isn't it?"

Opossum thanked Raccoon and scuttled away. First he built a fire. Next he wrapped bark strips around his furry tail. Then he stuck his tail right into the flame. Opossum instantly scorched off all his tail hair. The tail became bare.

Opossum wailed about his naked tail. All he could do was wait for new fur to grow back. And wait he did. But Opossum's tail was so badly burned that the fur never grew back. Opossum's tail remained bare for his entire life. And so it's been for opossums ever since.

1. Which word best describes Opossum?
   - ○ A. naked
   - ○ B. patient
   - ○ C. envious
   - ○ D. curious

2. What kind of text is this?
   - ○ A. nonfiction
   - ○ B. legend
   - ○ C. poetry
   - ○ D. drama

🌀 BrainTeaser 🌀

Write a synonym from the word bank for each boldface word below.

Word Bank

first
plain
tremble
concern
childish
supporter

1. **Humble** home _____

2. Team **sponsor** _____

3. **Initial** report _____

4. Mice **quiver** _____

5. Shows **courtesy** _____

6. **Juvenile** behavior _____

Reading & Math Practice, Grade 4 © 2014 Scholastic Inc.

Number Place

Order each set of numbers from *least* to *greatest*.

4,190   1,409   14,009 _____

12,007   21,700   12,707 _____

850,058   805,058   508,850 _____

21,000,000   12,200,000   210,200,000 _____

FAST Math

Subtract. Circle any answer whose digits add to 15.

```
    9,441           8,008            657
 -  3,283        -  6,337         -  278
 _____        _____         _____
```

```
    8,119             578          9,922
 -  4,822          -  499       -  4,625
 _____          _____       _____
```

Think Tank

Dodger Stadium in Los Angeles has 56,000 seats. The stadium in Florida where the Miami Marlins play has 36,331 seats. How many more seats are there in Dodger Stadium?

_____

Show your work in the tank.

Think Tank

Reading & Math Practice, Grade 4 © 2014 Scholastic Inc.

Data Place

Use the data in the calendar to answer the questions.

NOVEMBER

SUN	MON	TUE	WED	THU	FRI	SAT
		1	2	3	4	5
6	7	8	9	10	11	12
13	14	15	16	17	18	19
20	21	22	23	24	25	26
27	28	29	30			

1. Three dates in a row have a sum of 69. What are the dates?

   _____

2. Two dates in a row have a product of 132. What are the dates?

   _____

3. What is the product of dates on the

   2nd and 3rd Sundays? _____

4. What is the quotient when you divide the date of the last Wednesday

   by the first Saturday?_____

Puzzler

Figure out each code. Fill in the blanks.

1. $3 \times$ ♥ $+$ ◀ $= 11$ and ◀ $\times$ △ $= 10$.

   If ♥ $= 3$, then ◀ $=$ ____ and △ $=$ ____ .

2. $3 \times$ ☺ $-$ ☺ $=$ ✳ and ✳ $\times$ 🎁 $= 300$.

   If 🎁 $= 50$, then ✳ $=$ ____ and ☺ $=$ ____ .

Reading & Math Practice, Grade 4 © 2014 Scholastic Inc.

WORD of the Day

Use the word below in a sentence about separating a play area.

enclose: (v.) *to shut something in on all sides, surround*

_____

_____

Sentence Mender

Rewrite the sentence to make it correct.

They taken the bus to see there grandmother in kansas.

_____

Cursive Quote

Copy the quotation in cursive writing.

Prepare the umbrella before it rains.

—Malay proverb

- -

- -

- -

- -

What advice does this saying offer? Write your answer in cursive on another sheet of paper.

Analogy of the Day

Complete the analogy.

Orange is to **fruit** as _____ is to **vehicle**.

O A. car   O B. vegetable   O C. yellow   O D. driver

Explain how the analogy works: _____

_____

Ready, Set, READ!

Read the passage. Then answer the questions.

Making a Difference

It probably cheers you up to receive a card you didn't expect. Hannah Newton surely thought so. She was only seven, but she understood the joy that a happy surprise can bring.

Hannah turned this idea into an outreach project to help others. She thought it would be kind to send surprise cards to needy people. But she knew she couldn't do it alone. So she visited classrooms all over her area. She asked other kids to join her. Together they made cards with hopeful messages inside. She gathered over 800 surprise cards for people who needed a boost. Adults helped her deliver the cards wherever they could do the most good.

Hannah's idea has become the *Children Who Care Club*. Kids make cards each month to cheer up the homeless, the elderly, and the sick. She says, "Even though my age is small, my heart is big!"

1. What gave Hannah her idea to help others?

_____

_____

_____

_____

_____

2. Why might some elderly people need cheering up?

_____

_____

_____

_____

BrainTeaser

The word bank lists pioneer words. Each word is hidden in the puzzle. Find and circle each word.

Word Bank

BONNET
BUFFALO
CORNMEAL
HARDSHIP
HOMESTEAD
HUNGER
ILLNESS
JOURNALS
LANTERN
NAVIGATE

PIONEER
PRAIRIE
QUILT
RUMBLE
SCOUT
SUPPLIES
TRADERS
TRAIL
WAGON
YOKE

```
I L L N E S S R Y B H P O S
T R A I L Y W D N U O I T K
C O R N M E A L A F M O R R
R M C I S B E N V F E N A E
U P L C O I R R I A S E D G
K K O N R E U N G L T E E N
N U N I T M U T A O E R R U
T E A N B F Y P T K A E S H
T R A L D N A I E A D D V Y
P L E S L A N R U O J J S O
P I H S D R A H W A G O N K
S U P P L I E S T L I U Q E
```

Reading & Math Practice, Grade 4 © 2014 Scholastic Inc.

Number Place

Rewrite each number as only hundreds, only tens, or only ones.

Number	equals	Hundreds	or	Tens	or	Ones
400						
1,600						
9,000						
24,000						
410,000						

FAST Math

Subtract. Circle any answer that is greater than 50,000.

74,226 − 33,281	8,038 − 697	65,721 − 20,408
69,249 − 5,872	5,784 − 4,669	90,896 − 2,628

Think Tank

Jen is 26 years younger than her mom. Together, their ages total 50. How old is Jen?

_____

How old is her mom?

_____

Show your work in the tank.

Data Place

Students in Mantle School voted for their favorite baseball teams. The results are shown in the table.

Use the data to answer the questions.

1. Which team got 3 times as many votes as

   the Tigers did? _____

2. Which team got one-fourth as many

   votes as the Red Sox did? _____

3. One team got 5 times the number of votes another got. Name the teams.

   _____

Mantle's Favorite Teams

Team	Votes
Dodgers	84
Yankees	56
Red Sox	88
Phillies	36
Tigers	16
Marlins	22
Rangers	48
Cardinals	80

Puzzler

Work your way through the math maze from *Start* to *Finish*. Alternate addition and subtraction sentences. Use a straight line to connect the three numbers in each sentence. The first two are already done.

START

24	47	71	86	14	37	22
101	59	7	105	96	11	26
12	23	89	9	93	72	66
69	5	116	37	20	36	55
81	25	56	87	73	122	27
60	75	123	45	80	44	70
8	138	35	21	17	43	117

FINISH

Reading & Math Practice, Grade 4 © 2014 Scholastic Inc.

WORD of the Day

Use the word below in a sentence that tells about your favorite part of a movie, book, or TV show.

portion: (n.) *a part, or a share of something*

_____

_____

Sentence Mender

Rewrite the sentence to make it correct.

Would you likes budder or sour crime on you bake potato

_____

Cursive Quote

Copy the quotation in cursive writing.

There is no substitute for hard work.

—Thomas A. Edison

Do you think that Edison was right? Write your answer in cursive on another sheet of paper.

Analogy of the Day

Complete the analogy.

Skyscraper is to **tall** as _____ is to **sweet**.

○ A. pool   ○ B. sugary   ○ C. apartment   ○ D. candy

Explain how the analogy works: _____

_____

Ready, Set, READ!

Haiku is a form of poetry. It is often about nature, and it rarely rhymes. Haiku poets try to create one sharp image in very few words.

Read the haiku. Then answer the questions.

Four Haiku From Japan

For this lovely bowl
Let us arrange some flowers
Since there is no rice . . .
by Basho

Oh! I ate them all
And oh! What a stomach-ache . . .
Green stolen apples
by Shiki

Windy winter rain . . .
My silly big umbrella
Tries walking backward
by Shisei-Jo

You stupid scarecrow!
Under your very stick-feet
Birds are stealing beans!
by Yayu

1. Which word best describes the feeling in Yayu's haiku?
   ○ A. annoyance
   ○ B. ignorance
   ○ C. pleasure
   ○ D. curiosity

2. Basho suggests arranging flowers in the lovely bowl to
   ○ A. have a project.
   ○ B. decorate his home.
   ○ C. cover up rice stains.
   ○ D. avoid thinking of hunger.

3. Describe how Shisei-Jo's umbrella looks. _____

_____

BrainTeaser

Write the words from the word bank in alphabetical order in the rows of the grid. Circle the column that has another word for *speak*.

Word Bank

PEARL   CLOUD   HOSTS
KNEEL   FLUTE

Reading & Math Practice, Grade 4 © 2014 Scholastic Inc.

Number Place

Round each number to the nearest ten *and* hundred.

Number	Nearest 10	Nearest 100
617		
1,862		
4,345		
89,083		

FAST Math

Estimate each sum by rounding.

$$\begin{array}{r} 7{,}226 \\ +\ 3{,}381 \\ \hline \end{array} \qquad \begin{array}{r} 8{,}938 \\ +\ \ \ 797 \\ \hline \end{array} \qquad \begin{array}{r} 68{,}727 \\ +\ 21{,}008 \\ \hline \end{array}$$

$$\begin{array}{r} 509{,}849 \\ +\ 311{,}372 \\ \hline \end{array} \qquad \begin{array}{r} 5{,}724 \\ +\ 4{,}767 \\ \hline \end{array} \qquad \begin{array}{r} 888{,}056 \\ +\ 32{,}148 \\ \hline \end{array}$$

Think Tank

Inez has five coins that total $.60. What are the coins?

_____

_____

Show your work in the tank.

Data Place

Gracie and Will went to the SpaceFest. They got a schedule of events and talks at the Convention Center.

Use the schedule to answer the questions.

1. Which talk ends just before lunch?

   _____

2. Which talk lasts for 1 hour 15 minutes?

   _____

3. Which is the shortest talk?

   _____

Event	Start	End
Meet & Greet	8:30 A.M.	9:15 A.M.
Space Stations	9:20 A.M.	10:25 A.M.
Alien Life	10:30 A.M.	11:25 A.M.
Satellites	11:30 A.M.	12:20 P.M.
Lunch	12:25 P.M.	1:25 P.M.
Astronaut Training	1:30 P.M.	2:25 P.M.
Space Vacations	2:30 P.M.	3:45 P.M.
Space Art	3:40 P.M.	5:00 P.M.

4. Which is the longest talk? _____

5. Which two talks last for the same amount of time? _____

Puzzler

Each letter has a number value. Use the code to name an item that matches each of the descriptions below. Write the word and its value.

A = 1	B = 2	C = 3	D = 4	E = 5	F = 6	G = 7
H = 8	I = 9	J = 10	K = 11	L = 12	M = 13	N = 14
O = 15	P = 16	Q = 17	R = 18	S = 19	T = 20	U = 21
V = 22	W = 23	X = 24	Y = 25	Z = 26		

1. Animal with a sum between 20 and 30 _____

2. Food with a sum between 50 and 75 _____

3. Shape with a sum greater than 75 _____

Reading & Math Practice, Grade 4 © 2014 Scholastic Inc.

WORD of the Day

Use the word below in a sentence about something unusual that you have seen, tasted, heard, or done.

unique: (adj.) *one of a kind; rare, unusual, remarkable*

_____

_____

Sentence Mender

Rewrite the sentence to make it correct.

we muss start on time to finishing the game by dark

_____

Cursive Quote

Copy the quotation in cursive writing.

It's kind of fun to do the impossible.

—Walt Disney

- -

- -

- -

What can Disney mean by these words? Write your answer in cursive on another sheet of paper.

Analogy of the Day

Complete the analogy.

Piano is to **musician** as _____ is to **scientist**.

○ A. discovery   ○ B. microscope   ○ C. guitar   ○ D. glasses

Explain how the analogy works: _____

_____

Ready, Set, READ!

Read the passage. Then answer the questions.

Building an Igloo

An igloo is a dome-shaped hut made of blocks of hard snow. It has no corners. Inuit builders can make an igloo in about an hour. They work from the inside up. Here's how:

1. Pick a spot. Cut large blocks of icy snow. Make them about 3 feet wide, 2 feet tall, and 6 inches thick.

2. Stand in the hole left behind when you cut the blocks. Make a block circle around that hole. Tip each block inward a bit.

3. Now slice the tops off the first layer of blocks to start a big spiral. The lowest point meets the ground. The highest point is a full block tall.

4. Now add more blocks, starting from the lowest point. Spiral the blocks upward, and tip each block inward a bit. Keep spiraling around until the dome is almost closed.

5. Close the hole at the top by cutting a block to fit. Then chop out a door at the ground. Make it only as big as needed to crawl in and out.

1. How is an igloo different from other huts? _____

_____

_____

_____

2. Explain how the spiral helps shape the igloo and keep it standing.

_____

_____

_____

_____

_____

⊚ BrainTeaser ⊚

Find the extra word in each sentence and cross it out.

1. How many more chances do not we get?

2. Let's meet after school lets ends tomorrow.

3. This table spoon needs to be set for six people.

4. The noisy garbage bag truck woke me up at dawn.

5. Remember to take home your empty lunch money box.

Number Place

Round each number to its greatest place.

1,488 _____   435,456 _____

12,861 _____   922 _____

86,001 _____   277,005 _____

FAST Math

Round each number to its greatest place.
Then estimate each difference.

$$
\begin{array}{r} 71{,}826 \\ -\ 23{,}241 \\ \hline \end{array}
\qquad
\begin{array}{r} 6{,}038 \\ -\ 497 \\ \hline \end{array}
\qquad
\begin{array}{r} 668{,}721 \\ -\ 209{,}508 \\ \hline \end{array}
$$

$$
\begin{array}{r} 29{,}244 \\ -\ 4{,}892 \\ \hline \end{array}
\qquad
\begin{array}{r} 578{,}334 \\ -\ 416{,}009 \\ \hline \end{array}
\qquad
\begin{array}{r} 800{,}896 \\ -\ 27{,}528 \\ \hline \end{array}
$$

Think Tank

Anna's room is a rectangle. Its length is 15 feet and its width is 4 yards. What is the perimeter of the room?

_____

Show your work in the tank.

15 feet

4 yards

Think Tank

Data Place

LaTanya's family runs a small jewelry kiosk at the mall. The list shows the prices of some of the items they sell.

Use the price list to answer the questions.

Item	Price
Ring	$49.95
Bracelet	$34.99
Watch	$75.00
Earrings	$20.49
Necklace	$185.99

1. How much does it cost to buy 10 watches?

_____

2. How much more than a ring does a necklace cost? _____

3. Which items differ in price by about $40? _____

4. Lisa bought a bracelet and two watches. How much did she spend?

_____

5. Clark spent $70.44. Which 2 items did he buy? _____

Puzzler

Draw each point on the coordinate grid. Then connect them in order.

$$(2, 4) \rightarrow (6, 4) \rightarrow (8, 2) \rightarrow (4, 2) \rightarrow (2, 4)$$

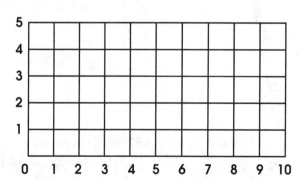

What kind of polygon did you make? _____

Reading & Math Practice, Grade 4 © 2014 Scholastic Inc.

WORD of the Day

Use the word below in a sentence about taking a photograph.

focus: (v.) *to adjust to create a clear image; to direct or fix on something*

_____

_____

Sentence Mender

Rewrite the sentence to make it correct.

Oh my goodness we won the raffle

_____

Cursive Quote

Copy the quotation in cursive writing.

Always be a little kinder than necessary.

—James M. Barrie

_____

_____

_____

What does this saying tell you about Barrie? Write your answer in cursive on another sheet of paper.

Analogy of the Day

Complete the analogy.

Cheerful is to **glad** as _____ is to **below**.

○ A. under   ○ B. above   ○ C. water   ○ D. thrilled

Explain how the analogy works: _____

_____

Ready, Set, READ!

Read the story. Then answer the questions.

Growing Pains

"Some dragon I am!" whined Valo. "All the other dragons breathe fire whenever they want. Some emit clouds of foul-smelling gas. But all I can manage is a cough."

"Valo, my scaly darling, you're still young," soothed his mother. "Your fire glands aren't mature enough. Have patience."

Valo had heard this explanation before, but he was weary of waiting. So he stomped around, hoping to speed up his growth. He rehearsed his roar, which was still peepy. He thrashed his tail in mock fury, splintering a few trees. He flew a bit and bashed some boulders, but no smoke, fire, or gas.

Valo came to a pasture of red peppers, the same color as his glowing eyes. In boredom, he nibbled a few of them. They were fiery hot peppers, which blistered his throat and made him gasp. The sting thrilled him, so he gorged himself on the whole crop! He ate so fast that he had to burp. When he did, an explosion of orange fire and rank air burst forth.

1. What is Valo's problem?

_____

_____

_____

_____

2. How does his mother try to calm him?

_____

_____

_____

_____

3. What kind of text is this?
- A. journal
- B. fantasy
- C. history
- D. myth

☾ BrainTeaser ☽

Write *a, e, i, o, u,* or *y* to finish spelling each instrument.

1. fl ___ t ___

2. h ___ rp

3. dr ___ ms

4. tr ___ mp ___ t

5. b ___ gp ___ p ___ s

6. tr ___ mb ___ n ___

7. ___ rg ___ n

8. r ___ c ___ rd ___ r

9. g ___ ___ t ___ r

10. t ___ mb ___ ___ r ___ n

Reading & Math Practice, Grade 4 © 2014 Scholastic Inc.

Number Place

Round to the place of the underlined digit.

<u>9</u>31,488 _____

<u>4</u>35,465 _____

192,8<u>6</u>6 _____

922,<u>0</u>07 _____

8<u>0</u>6,001 _____

23<u>7</u>,400 _____

FAST Math

Add or subtract.

$8.26
+ $3.41

$.38
− $.29

$87.06
+ $35.48

$912.44
− $48.92

$783.04
− $160.09

$218.26
+ $35.41

Think Tank

Kim's backyard is 9 meters wide. It is twice as long as it is wide. What is the perimeter of the yard?

_____

Show your work in the tank.

Data Place

What did your friends have for breakfast today?

Pick 4 breakfast items to count and tally. Then graph the results.

Breakfast Item	Tally

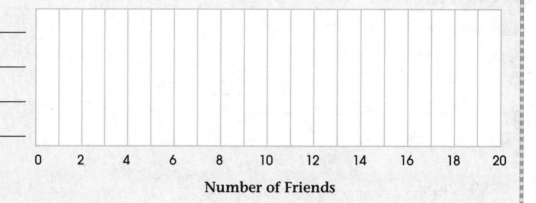

Breakfast Item

0   2   4   6   8   10   12   14   16   18   20

Number of Friends

What was hardest about this activity? _____

_____

Puzzler

Each problem has some missing digits.

**Use number sense to fill them in correctly.
Each of the digits 0–9 is missing only *once*.**

```
   2 6 □          1 1 □          6 □ 2          4 1 □          8 4 □
  − □ 3 8        + 5 2 6        − □ 3 7        + 1 8 7        −   8 3
  ───────        ───────        ───────        ───────        ───────
   1 2 7          6 □ 5          3 4 5          6 □ 3          □ 5 9
```

Reading & Math Practice, Grade 4 © 2014 Scholastic Inc.

WORD of the Day

Use the word below in a sentence about an ancient clay bowl.

artifact: (n.) *an object made by humans long ago, often a tool, ornament, or household item*

_____

_____

Sentence Mender

Rewrite the sentence to make it correct.

Keep all knifes away from small childs?

_____

Cursive Quote

Copy the quotation in cursive writing.

Play is not a luxury. Play is a necessity.

—Kay Redfield Jamison

What do you think makes play so necessary? Write your answer in cursive on another sheet of paper.

Analogy of the Day

Complete the analogy.

Page is to **book** as _____ is to **pencil**.

○ A. pen   ○ B. write   ○ C. desk   ○ D. eraser

Explain how the analogy works: _____

_____

Ready, Set, READ!

Read the interview. Then answer the questions.

Sub Grub   Dara interviews Jorge, U.S. Navy Culinary Specialist

Dara: *What exactly is a Culinary Specialist?*

Jorge: I'm a cook! On a submarine, like anywhere, people have to eat. But we can't just call in pizza!

Dara: *How's the food on submarines?*

Jorge: It's the best the Navy has to offer! Great food is our reward for all our sacrifices. We give up windows, fresh air, land, and space for months.

Dara: *What do you do besides cook?*

Jorge: Anything else the sub needs, and everything about food. The hardest part for a CS is the advance planning. I shop for three months of food, four meals a day, for the whole crew. Menus must be balanced, healthy, and not boring. Space is so tight that storage is a challenge, too.

Dara: *What foods are the crew's favorites?*

Jorge: Steak, lobster, and ice cream! We have a soft-serve ice cream machine, but it's not just for fun. Ice cream has calcium, eggs, and fruit.

1. What does CS stand for?
   ○ A. Crew Status
   ○ B. Calcium Service
   ○ C. Cook Sub
   ○ D. Culinary Specialist

2. Why does the Navy provide such great food for a submarine?

   _____

   _____

   _____

   _____

   _____

☺ BrainTeaser ☺

Complete the category chart. The letters above each column tell the first letter for each word. One word is done for you.

	B	**E**	**S**	**T**
Names of Cities		El Paso		
Map Words				
Forest Things				
Kitchen Things				

Number Place

Write each number in expanded form.

2,382 _____

40,306 _____

225,960 _____

600,010 _____

FAST Math ➡

Estimate each sum or difference.

$$\begin{array}{r} \$82.26 \\ +\ \$29.45 \\ \hline \end{array} \qquad \begin{array}{r} \$42.18 \\ -\ \ \$6.89 \\ \hline \end{array} \qquad \begin{array}{r} \$787.06 \\ +\ \$395.44 \\ \hline \end{array}$$

$$\begin{array}{r} \$622.42 \\ -\ \$278.92 \\ \hline \end{array} \qquad \begin{array}{r} \$783.04 \\ -\ \$160.09 \\ \hline \end{array} \qquad \begin{array}{r} \$218.26 \\ \$488.16 \\ +\ \ \$35.41 \\ \hline \end{array}$$

Think Tank

Teisha has 7 coins that add to $1. Only one of the coins is a dime. What are the coins?

_____

_____

_____

Show your work in the tank.

Reading & Math Practice, Grade 4 © 2014 Scholastic Inc.

73

Data Place

Make a Venn diagram with numbers between 0 and 50. Write multiples of 3 in one region. Write multiples of 5 in the other region. Write multiples of both 3 and 5 in the overlapping region.

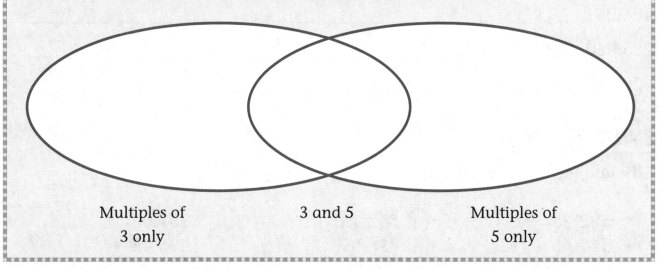

Multiples of
3 only

3 and 5

Multiples of
5 only

Puzzler

Fill in this design using 4 different colors. You can repeat colors—but not where sections touch.

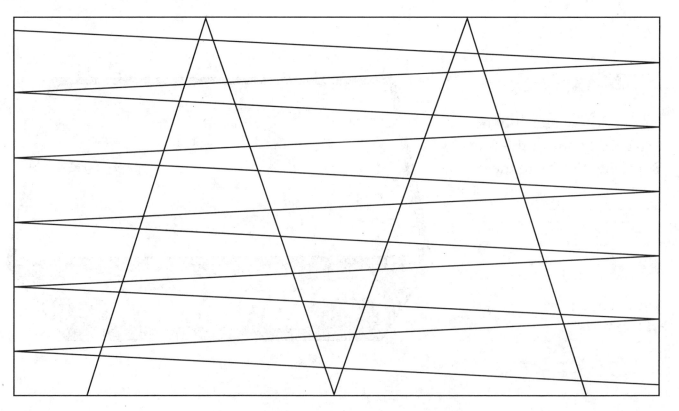

WORD of the Day

Use the word below in a sentence describing a fancy event.

lavish: (adj.) *far more than enough; beyond what is needed or expected; overly generous*

_____

_____

Sentence Mender

Rewrite the sentence to make it correct.

How do you say the word for homework? in spanish asked betsy.

_____

Cursive Quote

Copy the quotation in cursive writing.

You have to leave room in life to dream.

—Buffy Sainte-Marie

What makes dreaming worth your time? Explain your answer in cursive on another sheet of paper.

Analogy of the Day

Complete the analogy.

Teacher is to **faculty** as _____ is to **chorus**.

○ A. school   ○ B. night   ○ C. choir   ○ D. soprano

Explain how the analogy works: _____

_____

📖 Ready, Set, READ!

A *proverb* is a wise saying.

**Read the proverbs below, which warn of rain.
Then answer the questions.**

Will It Rain?

• Red sky in morning—sailors, take warning!
Red sky at night—sailor's delight.

• Thunder in morn, all day storm;
Thunder at night, traveler's delight.

• Catchy drawer and sticky door:
Coming rain will pour and pour.

• A ring around the sun or moon
Means rain or snow is coming soon.

• If grass is dry at morning light
Look for rain before the night.

• Ants that move their eggs and climb
Tell rain is coming anytime.

• When clouds look like smoke
A wise man wears his cloak.

1. What features do all these
proverbs share?

_____

_____

_____

_____

2. Which proverb sounds most
logical to you? Explain.

_____

_____

_____

_____

_____

_____

🌀 BrainTeaser 🌀

**Each sentence below has two blanks. Both use the same letters to form
different three-letter words. Fill them in. The first one is done for you.**

1. My _____ear_____ still hurts but my eyes _____are_____ fine.

2. _____ can we figure out _____ left the message?

3. After the storm, we _____ that there _____ a rainbow!

4. They _____ the first game, but who is ahead _____?

5. I am _____ sure how many pounds equal one _____.

6. Water ran into the _____ , _____ the drain was open!

Reading & Math Practice, Grade 4 © 2014 Scholastic Inc.

Number Place

Use all the numbers on the cards to form:

- the *greatest* number _____

- the *least* number _____

- the greatest *even* number _____

- the greatest *odd* number _____

6	1	5
2	7	3

FAST Math

Find each product as quickly as you can.

$3 \times 9 =$ _____ $5 \times 6 =$ _____ $7 \times 4 =$ _____

$5 \times 8 =$ _____ $4 \times 0 =$ _____ $4 \times 9 =$ _____

$6 \times 7 =$ _____ $1 \times 3 =$ _____ $7 \times 6 =$ _____

Think Tank

What is the perimeter of Tran's apartment?

_____

Show your work in the tank.

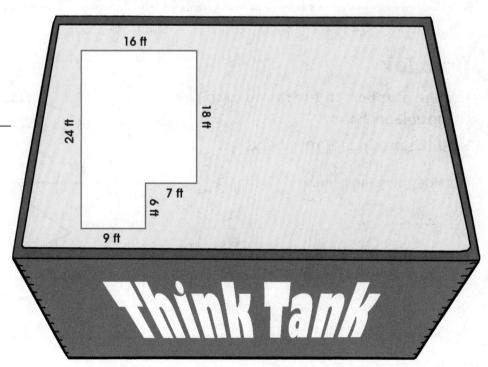

16 ft
18 ft
24 ft
7 ft
6 ft
9 ft

Data Place

Use the map of Veggie County to answer the questions.

All distances on the map are given in kilometers.

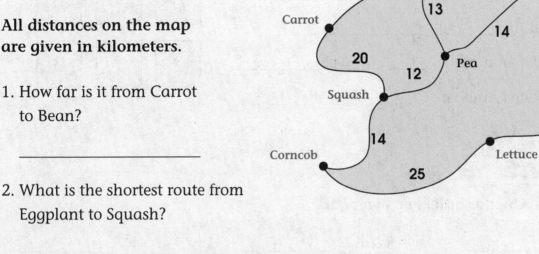

1. How far is it from Carrot to Bean?

   _____

2. What is the shortest route from Eggplant to Squash?

   _____

   How long is it? _____

3. Which two towns are 59 km apart one way and 77 km apart the other way?

   _____

Puzzler

Use the numbers in the figure to solve the problems below.

Find the product of numbers:

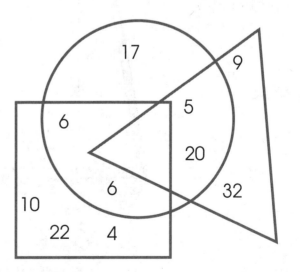

• inside the square *only*

   _____

• inside the triangle and circle

   _____

• inside the circle and square

   _____

Reading & Math Practice, Grade 4 © 2014 Scholastic Inc.

WORD of the Day

Use the word below in a sentence about a fair exchange you might make with a friend.

barter: (v.) *to trade objects or food for goods or services without using money; exchange*

_____

_____

Sentence Mender

Rewrite the sentence to make it correct.

Mom like chocolate covered cherrys better of all candy

_____

Cursive Quote

Copy the quotation in cursive writing.

A joy that's shared is a joy made double.

—Anonymous

_____

_____

_____

How can sharing spread more joy? Write your answer in cursive on another sheet of paper.

Analogy of the Day

Complete the analogy.

Lantern is to **light** as _____ is to **dig**.

○ A. bulb   ○ B. shovel   ○ C. hole   ○ D. rake

Explain how the analogy works: _____

_____

📖 Ready, Set, READ!

Read the passage. Then answer the questions.

Natural Pigment

The human eye can see millions of colors. Color pleases us and varies our world. Every culture uses color: people paint their skin, dye cloth, brighten up their homes, and make art.

Most natural materials have *pigment*—something in them that contains color. Did you ever get grass stains on your clothes? It came from pigment in the grass rubbing off on you. The first dyes may have been found by accidents just like that. Early people might have stained their skin or clothes with rock dust, food, or crushed plants. Over time, they learned to make dyes from nature's pigments. An important example of this is *cochineal*.

Grinding cochineal between stones

Cochineal comes from the crushed bodies of a beetle found in the Americas. Aztec and Mayan people would collect the beetles, drown them in hot water, dry them in the sun, and then crush them into a powder. Then they made the powder into a paste that could give yarn or cloth a deep red color. The powder has the same name as the insect it came from.

1. What is pigment? _____

_____

2. Cochineal is a kind of
   ○ A. culture   ○ B. plant   ○ C. cloth   ○ D. insect

🌀 BrainTeaser 🌀

Write all the different words you can spell using three or more letters from the word *conversation*.

_____

_____

_____

Reading & Math Practice, Grade 4 © 2014 Scholastic Inc.

Number Place

Read the clues to figure out the number.

- I am a 5-digit number.
- To the nearest ten-thousand, I round to 30,000.
- To the nearest thousand, I round to 27,000.
- To the nearest hundred, I round to 27,200.
- Four of my digits are 2s.

What number am I? _____

FAST Math

Find each product as quickly as you can.

$8 \times 9 =$ _____ $5 \times 9 =$ _____ $7 \times 7 =$ _____

$7 \times 8 =$ _____ $6 \times 0 =$ _____ $9 \times 7 =$ _____

$8 \times 1 =$ _____ $9 \times 9 =$ _____ $8 \times 6 =$ _____

Think Tank

Together, Iris and Ivan weigh 120 pounds. Iris weighs 10 pounds less than Ivan. How much does each child weigh?

_____

_____

Show your work in the tank.

Data Place

Use the graph to answer the questions about different pets students have.

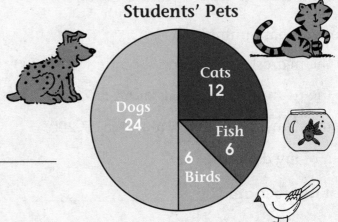

Students' Pets

Dogs 24
Cats 12
Fish 6
Birds 6

1. How many students have either a bird or a dog? _____

2. What kind of pet do $\frac{1}{4}$ of the students have? _____

3. How many times as many students have dogs as have fish? _____

4. Why is the dog part of the graph the largest? _____

_____

Puzzler

How many rectangles are there in this figure?

Describe how you organized your thinking.

_____

_____

_____

_____

WORD of the Day

Use the word below in a sentence about an example of this kind of writing that you enjoy reading.

prose: (n.) *ordinary style of text; writing that is not poetry*

_____

_____

Sentence Mender

Rewrite the sentence to make it correct.

Do you thought their will be a fire drill today!

_____

Cursive Quote

Copy the quotation in cursive writing.

Teach us to give and not to count the cost.

—Ignatius Loyola

How can there be different kinds of giving? Explain your idea in cursive on another sheet of paper.

Analogy of the Day

Complete the analogy.

Straw is to **drink** as _____ is to **reach**.

○ A. shelf   ○ B. milk   ○ C. ladder   ○ D. cup

Explain how the analogy works: _____

_____

📖 Ready, Set, READ!

Read the myth. Then answer the questions.

The Spirit Dog   *A Cherokee Myth*

The Cherokee depended on corn for food. They pounded it into meal for bread and mush. They stored it in large baskets.

At dawn one day, a woman went to her basket for cornmeal. She found a great mess. She noticed huge dog prints in the scattered cornmeal. They came from no ordinary dog. So she ran to the village and called the people together. She warned that a visit from a spirit dog was a bad sign. So the people agreed to scare the spirit dog so badly that it would never return.

That night everyone brought drums and rattles. They hid by the cornmeal and waited. Soon came a loud flapping sound. Looking up, they saw a huge dog flying in. It knocked over the baskets to get cornmeal. Just then, the people jumped up, beating drums and shaking rattles like thunder. The spirit dog ran off as the people and noise chased him.

At the top of a hill, the spirit dog leaped into the sky and flew into the darkness. Cornmeal fell from its mouth to form a faint path. Bits of cornmeal soon turned into stars.

1. What bad things might have happened if the spirit dog kept coming?

_____

_____

2. Many cultures have another name for the faint path the spirit dog made in the sky. Which name do you think it has in English?
   ○ A. Milky Way   ○ B. Great Dog   ○ C. Big Dipper   ○ D. Flying Fish

๑ BrainTeaser ๑

Each word below is missing the same letter from its beginning and end.
Complete every word using a *different* missing letter pair.

1. ____ indo ____

2. ____ noc ____

3. ____ an ____

4. ____ dg ____

5. ____ rus ____

6. ____ oya ____

7. ____ lum ____

8. ____ ealt ____

9. ____ ooste ____

Number Place

Round each money amount to the nearest dollar *and* ten dollars.

Amount	Nearest $1	Nearest $10
$6.17		
$28.62		
$843.45		

FAST Math

Break apart the factor in the rectangle to find the product.

$\boxed{7} \times 8 =$ (____ × 8) + (2 × 8) $\boxed{6} \times 7 =$ (5 × 7) + (____ × 7)

= ____ + 16   = 35 + ____

= 56   = 42

$\boxed{6} \times 9 =$ (____ × 9) + (____ × 9) $\boxed{7} \times 9 =$ (____ × 9) + (____ × 9)

= ____ + ____   = ____ + ____

= ____   = ____

Think Tank

Ari left the airport at 11:45 A.M. He drove for 55 minutes to get home. What time did he arrive?

_____

Show your work in the tank.

Think Tank

Data Place

Use the table about stadium seats to answer the questions.

Seats in a Stadium

Location	Number	Price
Field Level	8,000	$55
Mezzanine	5,600	$45
Loge	18,000	$35
Upper Deck	30,000	$25
Bleachers	800	$10

1. How many seats are in the stadium?

   _____

2. How many more seats are in the upper deck than in the loge?

   _____

3. What is the cost of 4 tickets in the mezzanine?

   _____

4. Cal bought 3 tickets for $105. Where are his seats? _____

5. Mia bought 2 tickets in one section and 2 in another. She spent $160 in all.

   Where are her seats? _____

Puzzler

Begin at the ★.

Skip count by 9s to connect the dots.

What picture did you make?

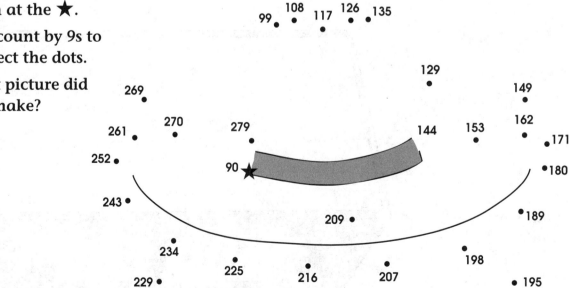

Reading & Math Practice, Grade 4 © 2014 Scholastic Inc.

WORD of the Day

Use the word below in a sentence about a sporting event or a debate.

agile: (adj.) *able to move quickly and easily; nimble; swift*

_____

_____

Sentence Mender

Rewrite the sentence to make it correct.

He watch in horror as a green snake creeped tword the tent

_____

Cursive Quote

Copy the quotation in cursive writing.

Reading is a discount ticket to everywhere.

—Mary Schmich

_____

_____

_____

What does Schmich mean by this statement? Write your answer in cursive on another sheet of paper.

Analogy of the Day

Complete the analogy.

Coal is to **dark** as _____ is to **hard**.

○ A. day   ○ B. floor   ○ C. soft   ○ D. sand

Explain how the analogy works: _____

_____

Ready, Set, READ!

Read the story. Then answer the questions.

The Ant Farm

A student describes her science project in a speech to her class.

You've all seen my ant farm in the back of our classroom. This is how I made it, care for it, and feel about it.

I got the idea online. So first, I collected backyard ants in a jar. I gathered dry dirt in another jar. I got an old picture frame from my mom to use as the farm. I figured I could watch the ants at work through the glass.

I put the dirt and then ants in. Once they were inside, I fed the ants tiny bits of fruit, veggies, and bread crumbs. I've also been feeding them dead flies and moths. I give them liquid by soaking a cotton ball in sugar water.

Many of you thought my ant farm was dumb, even disgusting at first. But soon I saw you staring at it. You watched my ants dig tunnels. You watched me feed and care for them. This makes me proud and my ants famous.

1. What is an ant farm? _____

_____

2. How did the attitude of the classmates change?

_____

_____

◎ BrainTeaser ◎

Use the clues to complete a word that starts with *pre*.

1. Hunter's victim   PRE ____

2. Squish   PRE ____ ____

3. Attractive   PRE ____ ____ ____

4. Choose over another   PRE ____ ____ ____

5. Make believe   PRE ____ ____ ____ ____

6. Forecast what may come   PRE ____ ____ ____ ____

7. Salty snack food   PRE ____ ____ ____ ____

88

Number Place

Round each money amount to the nearest $100 *and* $1,000.

Amount	Nearest $100	Nearest $1,000
$695.32		
$1,230.55		
$6,843.45		

FAST Math

Multiply.

$3 \times 40 = $ _____ $4 \times 50 = $ _____ $3 \times 80 = $ _____ $6 \times 30 = $ _____

$5 \times 70 = $ _____ $3 \times 400 = $ _____ $5 \times 600 = $ _____ $4 \times 500 = $ _____

$7 \times 300 = $ _____ $8 \times 600 = $ _____ $2 \times 900 = $ _____ $6 \times 700 = $ _____

Think Tank

What is the product of all numbers on a telephone key pad?

_____

Explain how you know.

_____

_____

_____

_____

Data Place

Use the graph about dog food in stock at Pam's Pets during a 5-week period to answer the questions.

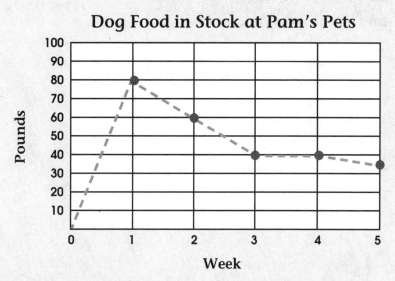

Dog Food in Stock at Pam's Pets

1. How many pounds of dog food did the store have in the first week? _____

   In the third week? _____

2. How much less dog food was in stock in the fourth week than in the second week?

   _____

3. Describe the change in the amount of dog food from weeks 1 to 5.

   _____

Puzzler

You will water Ms. Gold's plants each day for 10 days. She says, "I can pay you $10 a day. Or, I can pay you 25¢ the first day, and then double the amount each day after that."

Which plan should you take? Finish the table to help you decide.

Day	1	2	3	4	5	6	7	8	9	10
Pay	$.25	$.50	$1							

1. How much would you earn at $10 a day? _____

2. How much would you earn with the doubling plan? _____

90

WORD of the Day

Use the word below in a sentence about picking a team leader.

appoint: (v.) *to name to an office or position; officially choose or decide on*

_____

_____

Sentence Mender

Rewrite the sentence to make it correct.

be home bye for oclock said Dad

_____

Cursive Quote

Copy the quotation in cursive writing.

Champions keep playing until they get it right.

—Billie Jean King

- -

- -

- -

What do you think King, a tennis champion, means? Write your answer in cursive on another sheet of paper.

Analogy of the Day

Complete the analogy.

Carrot is to **vegetable** as _____ is to **planet**.

O A. Mars   O B. sun   O C. corn   O D. galaxy

Explain how the analogy works: _____

_____

Ready, Set, READ!

Read the passage. Then answer the questions.

Idaho Potatoes

We Idaho folk worship our potatoes. Idaho grows the biggest and finest ones anywhere. Out-of-staters can't believe it! A Utah cook once tried to buy a hundred pounds of potato from me, but I refused. "No, Ma'am!" I said. "I'd never sell just part of a potato. You buy a whole potato or none at all," I insisted.

Idaho potatoes are supremely tasty. They're the most buttery ones you'll ever eat. I suppose it's because we feed them like family: milk and cornmeal three times a day. Yeah, it must be that milk. Our potatoes are so creamy all you do is boil and mash them.

But Idaho potatoes aren't perfect. Our fields get so overcrowded you can hear grumbling from underground. "Roll over! You're squeezing me!" the 'taters complain. Then they poke up and cause problems on top. A guy I know got stuck for five hours under one pesky potato. His kids came looking for him when he didn't make it to supper. We all had to help drag him out.

1. What does the speaker suggest in his response to the Utah cook?

_____

_____

2. How does the picture support the speaker's claims?

_____

_____

⟲ BrainTeaser ⟳

Homophones are words that sound the same but have different spellings and meanings.
Write the correct word in each sentence.

1. Mom lets me _____ the turkey.   **baste** *or* **based**

2. Bears have thick, sharp _____.   **clause** *or* **claws**

3. Oh my, how tall they've _____!   **grown** *or* **groan**

4. Your library book is a week _____.   **overdo** *or* **overdue**

Number Place

Rewrite each money amount. Use $ and .

four dollars and sixty cents _____

twenty-seven dollars and thirty-four cents _____

one hundred ninety dollars and two cents _____

two thousand fifteen dollars and fifty cents _____

FAST Math

Multiply.

$8 \times 6{,}000 =$ _____ $6 \times 4{,}000 =$ _____ $3 \times 8{,}000 =$ _____

$4 \times 7{,}000 =$ _____ $5 \times 3{,}000 =$ _____ $8 \times 9{,}000 =$ _____

$9 \times 2{,}000 =$ _____ $7 \times 8{,}000 =$ _____ $8 \times 6{,}000 =$ _____

Think Tank

Rosa saw ducks and cows at a farm. In all, she counted 9 animals and 28 legs. How many ducks and how many cows did she see?

_____

_____

Show your work in the tank.

Data Place

The line plot shows the number of hours students said they spent reading each week.

Use the data in the line plot to answer the questions.

Hours Spent Reading

```
            X
            X
X           X
X   X   X   X
X   X   X   X
X   X   X   X   X
X   X   X   X   X   X
X   X   X   X   X   X                       X
─────────────────────────────────────────────
1   2   3   4   5   6   7   8   9   10
```

1. How many students were surveyed? _____

2. What is the range of the data? _____

3. What is the mode of the data? _____

4. How many students say they read for 5 hours each week? _____

5. An outlier is a value that "lies outside" (or away from) the rest of the data.

   Which number of hours is an outlier? _____

Puzzler

Complete the category chart. The letters above each column tell the first letter for each word. Three are done for you.

	R	O	P	E	S
Number Words	Roman numeral				
Measurement Words				equivalent	
Geometry Words			polygon		

Reading & Math Practice, Grade 4 © 2014 Scholastic Inc.

Reading & Math Practice, Grade 4 © 2014 Scholastic Inc.

WORD of the Day

Use the word below in a sentence to describe a key partner.

ally: (n.) *a person, group, or nation that agrees to support another to reach a shared goal; friend; partner*

_____

_____

Sentence Mender

Rewrite the sentence to make it correct.

The books silly titel make me laugh

_____

Cursive Quote

Copy the quotation in cursive writing.

It's not how big you are, it's how big you play.

—Anonymous

What can it mean to "play big"? Write your answer in cursive on another sheet of paper.

Analogy of the Day

Complete the analogy.

Mine is to **yours** as _____ is to **hers**.

O A. she   O B. him   O C. his   O D. he

Explain how the analogy works: _____

_____

📖 **Ready, Set, READ!**

Read the letter to the editor. Then answer the questions.

Dear Editor,

I read your newspaper sometimes. I like the section for suggesting ways to improve neighborhoods. People write about cleaning up parks, speeding up garbage pick-ups, improving mail delivery, and other subjects they think about. I'd like to add my two cents. My problem is with traffic lights.

I think the traffic lights on Central Avenue don't stay green long enough for the cross streets. My granddad walks me to school. We don't move so fast. If we don't start crossing Central just as the light turns green, we can barely get across in time. I don't think this is safe, and it's not fair. There are many older people and young kids where I live. We'd all benefit from longer light cycles. I think an extra 20 seconds of green would solve the problem.

Thank you for your attention.
Lynn Walker, age 8

1. What is the goal of Lynn's letter?
   - A. to complain
   - B. to add money
   - C. to get published
   - D. to adjust the light cycle

2. How would you describe her letter?
   - A. angry
   - B. lengthy
   - C. helpful
   - D. selfish

🌀 **BrainTeaser** 🌀

Unscramble each art word.
Write it correctly in the spaces.
Then unscramble the boxed letters to name an art product made with egg.

_____

PLATES ☐ _ _ ☐ _

REAMF _ _ ☐ _ _

YCAL _ ☐ _ _

LEFT _ ☐ _ _

NAPIT _ _ _ ☐

ORANYC _ ☐ _ _ _ _

Number Place

Compare. Write **<**, **=**, or **>**.

200,999 _____ 209,000 $\qquad$ 150,551 _____ 150,155

90,988 _____ 100,000 $\qquad$ 908,444 _____ 901,888

60,778 _____ sixty thousand seven hundred eighty-five

four hundred fifty thousand _____ 405,000

FAST Math

Round to the nearest 10 or 100. Then estimate the product.

$3 \times 68 =$ _____ $\qquad$ $6 \times 41 =$ _____ $\qquad$ $2 \times 807 =$ _____

$4 \times 771 =$ _____ $\qquad$ $5 \times 380 =$ _____ $\qquad$ $8 \times 915 =$ _____

$7 \times 27 =$ _____ $\qquad$ $9 \times 637 =$ _____ $\qquad$ $4 \times 662 =$ _____

Think Tank

Macaws can live to be about 64 years old. Hamsters live for about 4 years. About how many times longer than hamsters do macaws live?

_____

Show your work in the tank.

Data Place

The graph compares television sales at Ed's Electronics Store.

Use the graph to answer the questions.

Comparing Television Sales

Number of Sales — Television Size

2011 2012

1. Which size TV sold best in 2011? _____

2. Which size TV sold worst in 2012? _____

3. Which size TV had the greatest sales growth from 2011 to 2012? _____

4. How many more TVs sold in 2012 than in 2011? _____

Puzzler

Use the clues below to find out the home of the most famous groundhog in America.

____ ____ ____ ____ ____ ____ ____ ____ ____ ____ ____ ____ , PA

The second and sixth letters are *u*.

The fourth letter is *x*.

The third and tenth letters are *n*.

The eighth letter is *a*.

The twelfth letter is *y*.

The seventh letter is *t*.

The eleventh letter is *e*.

The ninth letter is *w*.

The first letter is *P*.

The fifth letter is *s*.

Reading & Math Practice, Grade 4 © 2014 Scholastic Inc.

WORD of the Day

Use the word below in a sentence that describes a photograph.

accurate: (adj.) *exactly right or correct; without error*

_____

_____

Sentence Mender

Rewrite the sentence to make it correct.

Strike tree yer out yelled the Umpire

_____

Cursive Quote

Copy the quotation in cursive writing.

A book is like a garden carried in the pocket.

—Chinese proverb

_____

_____

_____

_____

Why is a book compared to a garden? Explain your idea in cursive on another sheet of paper.

Analogy of the Day

Complete the analogy.

Sorry is to **regretful** as _____ is to **fragile.**

○ A. sturdy   ○ B. miserable   ○ C. lonely   ○ D. delicate

Explain how the analogy works: _____

_____

Reading & Math Practice, Grade 4 © 2014 Scholastic Inc.

Ready, Set, READ!

Read the letter. Then answer the questions.

23 April, 1846

Dearest Mother,

How I yearn for you, James, wee Emma, and our agreeable farm! Eight long months have passed since I came here to Lowell. Every afternoon I propose to write. But each day's work at the mill tires me mightily.

Share my thanks that I enjoy strong health. My wages bring in a decent three dollars per week. I share a modest room in a boarding house with five other girls. We are but ten minutes from the mill. Mrs. Howe provides a cold supper, though portions are woefully small.

Our overseer is a stern leader. We must report to the loom by five each morning. It is often cold and dark at that tender hour, but no matter. Our day includes two half-hour meal breaks. We stop work by seven most evenings.

I do not know when I shall visit. Perhaps for the turning of the new year? Winter travel may be hard, but I would endure a blizzard to see you all.

From your most affectionate daughter,

Mary

1. Why do you think Mary left home?

_____

_____

_____

_____

_____

_____

2. What is Mary's living situation now?

_____

_____

_____

_____

_____

_____

☙ BrainTeaser ☙

Write the words from the word bank in alphabetical order in the rows of the grid. Circle the column that has the name of a fictional character created by author Beverly Cleary.

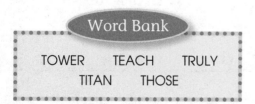

Word Bank

TOWER   TEACH   TRULY

TITAN   THOSE

Reading & Math Practice, Grade 4 © 2014 Scholastic Inc.

Number Place

Compare. Write **<**, **=**, or **>**.

$20,000 _____ $200,000 $150,500 _____ $150,150

$998,008 _____ $998,800 $90,999 _____ $900,000

$667,000 _____ six hundred seventy thousand dollars

four hundred five thousand dollars _____ $405,000

FAST Math

Round to the greatest place. Then estimate the product.

5 × 658 = _____   7 × 431 = _____   2 × 8,107 = _____

4 × 791 = _____   5 × 3,780 = _____   3 × 9,150 = _____

6 × 279 = _____   9 × 527 = _____   4 × 6,262 = _____

💡 Think Tank

There are 25 players on each Major League baseball team. There are 30 teams in all. How many players are in the Major Leagues?

_____

Show your work in the tank.

Data Place

Carlos rolled a 1–6 number cube 50 times. He recorded his results in a tally table.

Complete the bar graph to display the results.

Results for 50 Rolls

Number Rolled (y-axis: 1, 2, 3, 4, 5, 6)

Number of Rolls (x-axis: 0 2 4 6 8 10 12 14 16)

What I Rolled	How Many
1	卌 I
2	IIII
3	卌 卌 II
4	卌 卌 III
5	卌 卌 II
6	III

1. Which two numbers came up the same number of times? _____

2. Which number came up the most often? _____

Puzzler

Each number has a different shape around it in the tic-tac-toe grid. For instance, ⌐ stands for 8. Do you see why?

Use this code to solve the problems.

1	2	3
4	5	6
7	8	9

1. ⌐ ⌐ × ⌐ = _____

2. ⌐ ⌐ × ⌐ = _____

3. ⌐ ⌐ ⌐ × ⌐ = _____

4. ⌐ ⌐ ⌐ ⌐ × ⌐ = _____

WORD of the Day

Use the word below in a sentence about an accident.

collide: (v.) *to crash or bump into; to strike, hit, or come together with force*

_____

_____

Sentence Mender

Rewrite the sentence to make it correct.

I knows all the words to all five verse's of This land is your land

_____

Cursive Quote

Copy the quotation in cursive writing.

When the mind is thinking, it is talking to itself.

—Plato

. . . .

. . . .

. . . .

Do you agree with Plato? Explain. Write your answer in cursive on another sheet of paper.

Analogy of the Day

Complete the analogy.

Green is to **color** as _____ is to **spice**.

○ A. ketchup   ○ B. red   ○ C. cinnamon   ○ D. lemon

Explain how the analogy works: _____

_____

 Ready, Set, READ!

Read the recipe. Then answer the questions.

Whip up a dozen homemade soft pretzels!

Ingredients
$\frac{1}{3}$ cup baking soda
5 cups water
3 cups flour
1 teaspoon baking soda
$\frac{1}{4}$ cup honey
1 cup buttermilk
Coarse salt

Utensils
• Cookie sheet
• Cooking spray
• Measuring cups
• Non-aluminum cooking pot
• Pot holder
• Large mixing bowl and spoon

What to Do
1. Preheat oven to 400°F.
2. Grease cookie sheet with cooking spray.
3. Mix $\frac{1}{3}$ cup baking soda and water in pot. Boil, then let cool.
4. In bowl, blend flour and 1 tsp. baking soda. Add honey and buttermilk. Stir to form dough. Knead on a floured surface for 1 minute.
5. Divide dough into 12 equal pieces. Roll out each piece into a "snake" about 1 foot long. Twist into a pretzel knot. Pinch ends together.
6. Dip pretzels in baking soda water. Place on cookie sheet.
7. Sprinkle pretzels with salt. Bake until golden (about 10 minutes).

1. Why is baking soda listed twice?

_____

_____

_____

_____

2. What does it mean to *knead* dough? _____

_____

_____

_____

BrainTeaser

Write an antonym from the word bank for each boldface word below.

1. **Vacant** chair _____

2. **Previous** week _____

3. Plants **wither** _____

4. **Frantic** shoppers _____

5. **Sincere** smile _____

Word Bank
calm
false
blossom
occupied
following

104

Reading & Math Practice, Grade 4 © 2014 Scholastic Inc.

Number Place

Write any number that belongs between.

2,140 < _____ < 2,150   51,400 > _____ > 51,395

7,065 < _____ < 7,100   60,001 > _____ > 59,998

89,000 < _____ < 89,003   30,078 > _____ > 30,000

FAST Math

Find each product. Circle the two products that are the same.

5 × 56 = _____   4 × 91 = _____   4 × 19 = _____

6 × 702 = _____   6 × 316 = _____   8 × 68 = _____

3 × 922 = _____   7 × 52 = _____   7 × 751 = _____

Think Tank

Forty-four runners from Thorpe School are going to a track meet. The vans that take them hold 8 students each. How many vans do the runners need?

_____

Show your work in the tank.

Data Place

The Fish Tank is having a sale on some popular items.

Use the price list to answer the questions below.

1. How much more than the book

   does the tank cost? _____

2. Jae spent $29.73 on three items. What

   are they? _____

   _____

3. Which costs more: 2 of the 20-gallon tanks

   or 6 sunken ships? _____

   _____

   How much more? _____

Item	Price
Fish Food	$ 5.79
Tropical Fish Book	$15.25
Tank Plant	$10.99
20-Gallon Tank	$35.95
Sunken Ship	$12.95

Puzzler

In each shape, cross out the fraction or mixed number that does *not* belong.
Then, write one that *does* belong on the line beneath the shape.

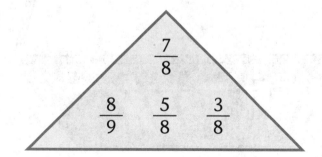

$\frac{7}{8}$

$\frac{8}{9}$ $\frac{5}{8}$ $\frac{3}{8}$

$1\frac{4}{8}$ $1\frac{3}{6}$

$1\frac{2}{5}$ $1\frac{5}{10}$

1. _____

2. _____

Reading & Math Practice, Grade 4 © 2014 Scholastic Inc.

WORD of the Day

Use the word below in a sentence about lack of rain on a farm.

drought: (n.) *a long period of dry weather; extended time with little or no rain*

_____

_____

Sentence Mender

Rewrite the sentence to make it correct.

Arthur wynne make the 1st crossword puzzel in 1913

_____

Cursive Quote

Copy the quotation in cursive writing.

Once you learn to read, you will be forever free.

—Frederick Douglass

_____

_____

_____

_____

Douglass was born into slavery. Though it was against the law, he learned to read. How do those facts help explain the quotation? Respond in cursive on another sheet of paper.

Analogy of the Day

Complete the analogy.

Brake is to **stop** as _____ is to **cut**.

○ A. horn   ○ B. scissors   ○ C. slice   ○ D. tire

Explain how the analogy works: _____

_____

📖 **Ready, Set, READ!**

Read the lyrics. Then answer the questions.

My Grandfather's Clock *Traditional Folksong*

My grandfather's clock was too large for the shelf
So it stood ninety years on the floor.
It was taller by half than the old man himself
Though it weighed not a pennyweight more.
It was bought on the morn of the day that he was born
And was always his treasure and pride.
But it stopped short—never to go again—
When the old man died.

> Ninety years without slumbering (tick tock tick tock)
> His life's seconds numbering (tick tock tick tock)
> It stopped short—never to go again—
> When the old man died.

1. If the man was 6 feet tall, how tall was the clock? _____

_____

2. What was so remarkable about this clock? _____

_____

🌀 **BrainTeaser** 🌀

The word wheel holds nine letters. If you use all nine
of them, you can form a nine-letter word about books.
Form other words (from three to eight letters), always
using the R in the center and any others.

_____

_____

_____

_____

Reading & Math Practice, Grade 4 © 2014 Scholastic Inc.

Number Place

Write the next 2 numbers in each pattern.

33   303   3,003   _____   _____

7,001   8,001   9,001   _____   _____

204   2,005   20,006   _____   _____

1,000,009   100,008   10,007   _____   _____

FAST Math

Multiply. Circle the two products that have a sum of 925.

5 × 36 = _____   4 × 98 = _____   4 × 397 = _____

6 × 752 = _____   6 × 816 = _____   8 × 78 = _____

3 × 622 = _____   7 × 43 = _____   5 × 671 = _____

Think Tank

Leon ordered two items from the catalog. His change from a $20 bill was $6.10. Which two items did he order?

_____

_____

Show your work in the tank.

COSTUME SUPPLIES	
Top Hat	$ 4.79
Mask	$ 8.95
Bag of Eyeballs	$ 3.95
Whistle	$ 2.95
Fake Fangs	$ 4.19
Clown Shoes	$ 9.95

Think Tank

Data Place

Identify the coordinates for each ordered pair that forms the
square. Write them on the line below each grid.

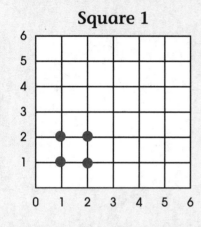
Square 1

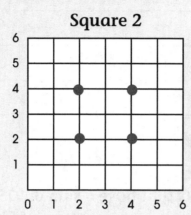
Square 2

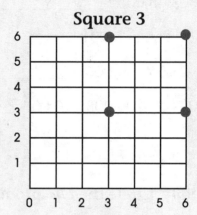
Square 3

_____   _____   _____

Compare the coordinates of the first and third squares.

What pattern do you notice? _____

_____

Puzzler

The triangles have 9 boxes. Use the numbers 1–9 once
in each triangle. Write a number in each box so that
the sum on each side of the triangle is the same.

1. Make the *least* possible sum.   2. Make the *greatest* possible sum.

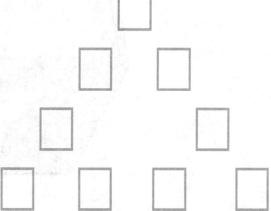

WORD of the Day

Use the word below in a sentence about an annoying sound.

constant: (adj.) *not stopping; always the same; unchanging*

_____

_____

Sentence Mender

Rewrite the sentence to make it correct.

Nineth president William henry Harrison serve for less then thirty-one day

_____

Cursive Quote

Copy the quotation in cursive writing.

One kind word can warm three winter months.

—Japanese saying

_____

_____

_____

What do you think this saying means? Write your answer in cursive on another sheet of paper.

Analogy of the Day

Complete the analogy.

Bottom is to **top** as _____ is to **left**.

○ A. leave   ○ B. up   ○ C. center   ○ D. right

Explain how the analogy works: _____

_____

📖 Ready, Set, READ!

Read the passage. Then answer the questions.

One of a Kind

Jim Abbot was an amazing athlete. His best sport was baseball. This lefty pitcher was a star in high school and in college. In 1987, he won the Sullivan Award as the nation's best amateur athlete. He pitched in the Olympics in 1988.

Abbot reached the major leagues in 1989. He won 87 games in his career. He even threw a no-hitter, which is rare for any pitcher.

When he pitched, Abbot did something other pitchers did not. He kept his glove tucked under his right arm. Once he released the ball, he slipped his hand into the glove to prepare to catch the ball if it came his way. If it did, he would catch it and quickly remove the ball from the glove in time to throw it. He did this smoothly and accurately.

Jim Abbot followed this routine with every pitch he made. Why? He did it because he had to. Abbot was born without a right hand.

1. Which word is the opposite of *amateur*?

   ○ A. adult   ○ B. professional   ○ C. beginner   ○ D. part-time

2. Why did Abbot pitch and field differently than other pitchers?

   _____

   _____

🌀 BrainTeaser 🌀

Use the clues to write a word that includes z.

1. Not hard working   ___ ___ Z ___

2. Feeling comfy and warm   ___ ___ Z ___

3. Flavorful and spicy   Z ___ ___ ___ ___

4. Group of 12 things   ___ ___ Z ___ ___

5. Gentle wind   ___ ___ ___ ___ Z ___

6. Four-legged reptile   ___ ___ Z ___ ___ ___

Number Place

Write the correct number from the box.

• It is the greatest number. _____

• They are less than 8,000.

_____

• They are greater than 80,000

_____

• Circle the leftover numbers.

3,811	9,005
10,500	
8,005	20,530
101,005	
100,500	85,875
4,981	

FAST Math

Find each product. Circle any product that rounds to $3.

8 × $.45 = _____   7 × $.40 = _____   1 × $7.00 = _____

6 × $2.23 = _____   4 × $5.20 = _____   2 × $8.55 = _____

9 × $3.39 = _____   3 × $.67 = _____   5 × $9.82 = _____

Think Tank

Brian's team scored 26 two-point baskets and 7 three-point baskets. How many points did his team score?

_____

Show your work in the tank.

Data Place

Forty-eight students took a homework survey. The table shows the results. But some of the table is blank.

Use the clues to complete the table.

- Four times as many students prefer working on the floor to working on the bed.

- Seven times as many students prefer working at a table to working on the bed.

Best Homework Spot	Tally	Number
	IIII	
		16

Puzzler

Tetrominoes are figures made of 4 squares joined flush along 1 or more sides. Two have been done as examples.

Draw four other tetrominoes on the grid.

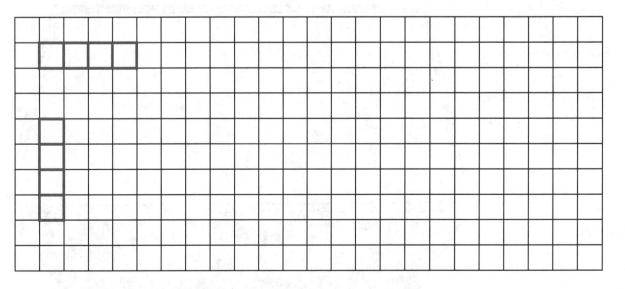

Reading & Math Practice, Grade 4 © 2014 Scholastic Inc.

WORD of the Day

Use the word below in a sentence about leaving a door open.

neglect: (v.) *to forget or give too little attention to*

_____

_____

Sentence Mender

Rewrite the sentence to make it correct.

My unkle always sing a dum song called the eggplant that ate chicago

_____

Cursive Quote

Copy the quotation in cursive writing.

You always pass failure on the way to success.

—Mickey Rooney

. . . .

. . . .

. . . .

How can failure now lead to success later? Explain your idea in cursive on another sheet of paper.

Analogy of the Day

Complete the analogy.

Simple is to **challenging** as _____ is to **create**.

○ A. easy   ○ B. destroy   ○ C. invest   ○ D. difficult

Explain how the analogy works: _____

_____

Ready, Set, READ!

Read the passage. Then answer the questions.

The Dog and His Reflection
by Aesop

A hungry dog was searching for a meal. Soon he came upon a sizable piece of meat. Overjoyed by his luck, he decided to carry the meat back to his den to eat in peace and comfort. On his way there, he loped proudly across a bridge over a stream. As he crossed, he looked down into the water. There he saw his own reflection. But the dog believed he was seeing another dog holding an even bigger piece of meat. His belly rumbled, but he paused to consider what to do.

He decided to steal the other dog's meat. But as he opened his mouth to do this, his own piece of meat fell. It splashed into the stream and was swept away. The dog lost his treasure and was left with only his hunger.

1. What does *overjoyed* mean?
   - ○ A. too happy
   - ○ B. unhappy
   - ○ C. happy again
   - ○ D. very happy

2. What lesson does this fable attempt to teach?

   _____

   _____

   _____

   _____

   _____

   _____

๑ BrainTeaser ๑

Write *a, e, i, o, u,* or *y* to finish spelling each baseball word.

1. ___ nn ___ ng

2. str ____ k ____

3. sl ____ gg ____ r

4. b ___ nt

5. gl ____ v ____

6. s ___ ngl ____

7. st ____ ____ l

8. tr ____ pl ____

9. m ____ ____ nd

10. f ____ ____ ld ____ r

11. t ____ g

12. sl ____ d ____

13. ____ ____ t

14. c ____ tch ____ r

Reading & Math Practice, Grade 4 © 2014 Scholastic Inc.

Number Place

Write the decimal for each part.

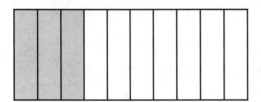

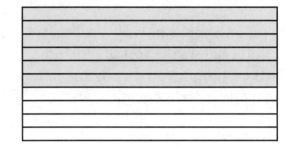

_____   _____

FAST Math

Find each quotient as quickly as you can.

27 ÷ 3 = _____   18 ÷ 2 = _____   32 ÷ 4 = _____

30 ÷ 3 = _____   24 ÷ 4 = _____   0 ÷ 5 = _____

40 ÷ 5 = _____   30 ÷ 3 = _____   36 ÷ 4 = _____

Think Tank

Rosa's teacher ordered 6 pizzas for a party. Each cost $12.75. She shared the cost equally with 4 other teachers. How much did each teacher pay?

_____

Show your work in the tank.

Data Place

Sue's Sign Shop is having a sale. The table shows the cost of placing words on a sign. You pay by the letter. Prices vary by letter heights.

Use the table to answer the questions.

Letter Height	Price per Letter
1 inch	$.75
3 inches	$1.50
6 inches	$2.75
9 inches	$4.00
12 inches	$5.50

1. What would it cost for a sign with your first and last names in 3-inch letters? _____

2. What would it cost for a sign with the name of your school in 12-inch letters? _____

3. Alex got a sign that says VOTE FOR ME. He spent $24.75. What size letters did he get? _____

Puzzler

Choose one number from each box to find each product.

Box A

	316	649
88	447	205

Box B

	5	4
3	6	2

1. _____ × _____ = 2,235
   A   B

2. _____ × _____ = 1,264
   A   B

Reading & Math Practice, Grade 4 © 2014 Scholastic Inc.

WORD of the Day

Use the word below in a sentence about asking a favor.

response: (n.) *a reply; any answer given in words or by actions*

_____

_____

Sentence Mender

Rewrite the sentence to make it correct.

Jamille past the test and got the higher score of enybody

_____

Cursive Quote

Copy the quotation in cursive writing.

If we cannot be clever, we can always be kind.

—Alfred Fripp

_____

_____

_____

Do you think that Fripp's words make sense? Explain your idea in cursive on another sheet of paper.

Analogy of the Day

Complete the analogy.

Wheel is to **bicycle** as _____ is to **pie**.

○ A. sweet   ○ B. fruit   ○ C. cake   ○ D. shape

Explain how the analogy works: _____

_____

 **Ready, Set, READ!**

Read the passage. Then answer the questions.

A Flood of Bats

Bracken Bat Cave is near San Antonio, Texas. It is the summer home to more than 20 million Mexican free-tailed bats. From March to October, Bracken holds one of the greatest mammal populations on earth.

Interested visitors can witness a Bracken Bat Flight. This outdoor event lasts between three and four hours. Keep these points in mind as you plan your visit:

• Bat Flights take place rain or shine. Dress for the weather and for rugged, dusty conditions near the cave.

• You may bring binoculars and cameras, but flash use is not allowed. You may not bring chairs, food, or pets.

• Bats are wild animals. They emerge nightly to hunt insects. But the exact time is unknown. It can take up to three hours for all bats to exit the cave.

• Bats are highly sensitive to noise. Remain as quiet as possible, and stay on the hillside near the cave.

1. What kind of animal is a bat?

　○ A. reptile　　○ B. bird　　○ C. amphibian　　○ D. mammal

2. Which is *not* allowed at a Bracken Bat Flight?

　○ A. feeding　　○ B. sleeping　　○ C. observing　　○ D. standing

⑨ BrainTeaser ⑥

What did the porcupine ask the cactus?

Solve each clue. Then copy each letter into its numbered box to find the answer to the riddle.

• Card game

　$\overline{}_{2}$ $\overline{}_{6}$ $\overline{}_{11}$ $\overline{}_{7}$ $\overline{}_{8}$

• Pirate "yes"

　$\overline{}_{1}$ $\overline{}_{4}$ $\overline{}_{3}$

• Cow sound

　$\overline{}_{9}$ $\overline{}_{5}$ $\overline{}_{10}$

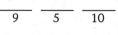
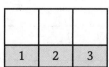
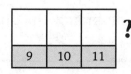

| 1 | 2 | 3 | | 4 | 5 | 6 | | 7 | 8 | | 9 | 10 | 11 | ? |

Reading & Math Practice, Grade 4 © 2014 Scholastic Inc.

Number Place

Write the decimal for each part.

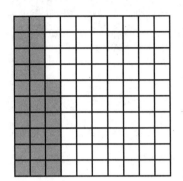

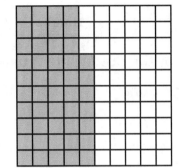

_____

_____

FAST Math

Find each quotient as quickly as you can.

24 ÷ 6 = _____   56 ÷ 7 = _____   36 ÷ 6 = _____

48 ÷ 6 = _____   49 ÷ 7 = _____   0 ÷ 6 = _____

42 ÷ 7 = _____   42 ÷ 6 = _____   63 ÷ 7 = _____

Think Tank

The average mass of a cat's brain is 3.3 grams. That is 0.8 grams more than the average rabbit brain. What is the mass of the average rabbit brain?

_____

Show your work in the tank.

Data Place

Nita runs a kennel. The table shows the kinds of dogs at the kennel today.

Dog Breed	Boxer	Collie	Hound	Mutt	Terrier
Number	28	32	30	48	22

Make a pictograph of the data. Give it a title and a key.

Use 🐾 to stand for 4 dogs.

_____

Boxer	
Collie	
Hound	
Mutt	
Terrier	
Key 🐾 = _____ dogs	

Puzzler

Use the fraction code to spell two different math words.
Write the letters in the order they appear in the clue.

The last $\frac{2}{5}$ of **triad**

The last $\frac{1}{3}$ of **parade**

The middle $\frac{1}{3}$ of **wander**

_____

The last $\frac{1}{5}$ of **catch**

The last $\frac{1}{2}$ of **apex**

The first $\frac{1}{3}$ of **agreed**

The second $\frac{2}{3}$ of **son**

_____

Make up your own fraction code to spell your last name. Use another sheet of paper.

122

Reading & Math Practice, Grade 4 © 2014 Scholastic Inc.

WORD of the Day

Use the word below in a sentence about a yearly event you enjoy.

annual: (adj.) *happening or coming once a year*

_____

_____

Sentence Mender

Rewrite the sentence to make it correct.

Wear were you on Saturday june 16 2012 dr miller?

_____

Cursive Quote

Copy the quotation in cursive writing.

I learned the value of hard work by working hard.

—Margaret Mead

- -

- -

- -

Why do so many successful people praise hard work? Write your answer in cursive on another sheet of paper.

Analogy of the Day

Complete the analogy.

Cracker is to **crispy** as _____ is to **gritty**.

○ A. sand   ○ B. cookie   ○ C. creamy   ○ D. gravy

Explain how the analogy works: _____

_____

Ready, Set, READ!

Read the passage. Then answer the questions.

Man and Dog

A man and his dog enter a diner and sit at the counter. The man tells the server that his dog can talk. "No way," the server replies.

"Way," the man answers. "Just listen!" He asks his dog to say what is atop every house.

"Roof," the dog barks. The server is unimpressed. So the man asks his dog another question.

"How does sandpaper feel?"

"Ruff," the dog barks. Still the server is unconvinced.

"Come on," she says. "Your dog can't talk any more than mine can."

"Usually you can't shut her up," the man insists. "Let me try again." Turning to his dog, he asks, "Molly, who is the best ball player ever?"

"Roof," answers Molly, wagging her tail in triumph. The server turns away, shaking her head. The man and the dog leave. Outside, Molly taps her owner with her large paw and asks, "Should I have said *Babe* Roof?"

1. What is the dog's name? _____

2. What makes this joke funny? _____

_____

⑨ BrainTeaser ⑥

Think of one word that all three words on the left have in common.
Write it on the line. The first one is done for you.

1. wagon
   cart   <u>wheel</u>
   Ferris

2. tree
   circus   _____
   diamond

3. spider
   world-wide _____
   Charlotte's

4. picnic
   waste   _____
   Easter

5. baby
   olive   _____
   engine

6. pig
   ball-point _____
   fountain

Reading & Math Practice, Grade 4 © 2014 Scholastic Inc.

Number Place

Circle each number that has a 4 in the tenths place.

4.5   7.4   23.04   40.43

Circle each number that has a 4 in the hundredths place.

4.05   7.14   24.04   30.47

Circle each number that does not have a 4 in the tenths or hundredths place.

4.01   7.14   84.04   40.32

FAST Math

Find each quotient as quickly as you can.

$32 \div 8 =$ _____ $36 \div 9 =$ _____ $40 \div 10 =$ _____

$63 \div 9 =$ _____ $45 \div 9 =$ _____ $64 \div 8 =$ _____

$60 \div 10 =$ _____ $48 \div 8 =$ _____ $56 \div 8 =$ _____

Think Tank

Jada bought a 64-ounce container of apple juice. How many full 6-ounce glasses of juice can she serve her friends?

_____

Show your work in the tank.

Reading & Math Practice, Grade 4 © 2014 Scholastic Inc.

Data Place

Students named the continent they most want to visit.

Use the graph to answer the questions.

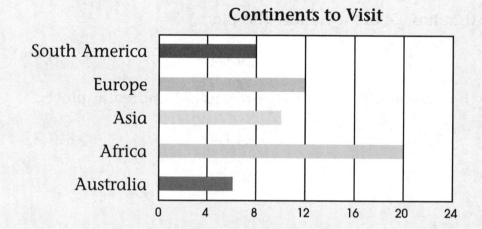

Continents to Visit

1. How many students voted? _____

2. Which continent got more than twice the number of votes South America did?

   _____

3. How many more students chose Africa than Europe? _____

Puzzler

Draw a picture to help you solve this money puzzle.

Matsu put 12 pennies in a row on his desk.

Then he swapped every 2nd penny for a quarter.

Next, he swapped every 3rd coin for a dime.

Finally, he swapped every 4th coin for a nickel.

1. How much money is on the desk now?

_____

2. How much more is it than Matsu started with?

_____

126

Reading & Math Practice, Grade 4 © 2014 Scholastic Inc.

WORD of the Day

Use the word below in a sentence to tell why you do not support a certain rule or plan.

oppose: (v.) *to be or act against something; fight or resist*

_____

_____

Sentence Mender

Rewrite the sentence to make it correct.

Can you belive that alaska has a town called y?

_____

Cursive Quote

Copy the quotation in cursive writing.

Don't look where you fall, but where you slipped.

—African proverb

- -

- -

What is the meaning of this proverb? Write your answer in cursive on another sheet of paper.

Analogy of the Day

Complete the analogy.

Driver is to **car** as _____ is to **train**.

O A. pilot   O B. caboose   O C. track   O D. engineer

Explain how the analogy works: _____

_____

📖 Ready, Set, READ!

Read the passage. Then answer the questions.

Didjeridu

The didjeridu may be the world's oldest wind instrument. It is mainly a hollow wooden tube. It is played by blowing into it while buzzing the lips. The "didj" is also called a wooden trumpet, drone pipe, or yidaki. The first didj was made by the Aborigines of northern Australia. They used it during ceremonies.

A traditional didj was made of a eucalyptus sapling or branch. Termites naturally eat out the inside of the tree over the course of about a year. Didj makers harvest the wood when they find one of just the right thickness. They cut it to any length they choose, based on the sound they want. Shorter lengths play higher tones; longer lengths player lower tones.

Didj makers usually strip away the outer bark and clean out all the termites. Some smooth or carve the outside. Many use wax to form a soft mouthpiece that has an airtight seal. The didj may be painted or left natural.

1. What kind of instrument is the didjeridu?

   ○ A. rhythm   ○ B. wind   ○ C. string   ○ D. brass

2. Explain how the length of a didj affects its sound. _____

_____

🌀 BrainTeaser 🌀

Go on a word hunt—from your seat! Write an item that includes each word part listed below. Look around the room and out the window for ideas. Words can be any length.

Word part	Item
1. ain	
2. atch	
3. eed	
4. ase	
5. ime	

Word part	Item
6. ish	
7. old	
8. ox	
9. ound	
10. one	

Reading & Math Practice, Grade 4 © 2014 Scholastic Inc.

Number Place

Write each decimal in number form.

three tenths _____

seven hundredths _____

sixty-two hundredths _____

sixteen hundredths _____

nine tenths _____

one hundredth _____

FAST Math

Find the missing numbers.

If 3 × 9 = 27, then 3 × 90 = _____ .

If 6 × 8 = _____ , then 6 × 80 = _____ .

If 7 × 7 = _____ , then 7 × 70 = _____ and 7 × 700 = _____ .

If 35 ÷ 5 = 7, then 350 ÷ 5 = _____ .

If 54 ÷ 9 = _____ , then 540 ÷ 9 = _____ .

If 32 ÷ 4 = _____ , then 320 ÷ 4 = _____ and 3,200 ÷ 4 = _____ .

Think Tank

An oak tree is 5.5 meters tall. An elm tree is 1.1 meters shorter. How tall is the elm tree?

_____

Show your work in the tank.

Data Place

Use the graph about building heights to answer the questions.

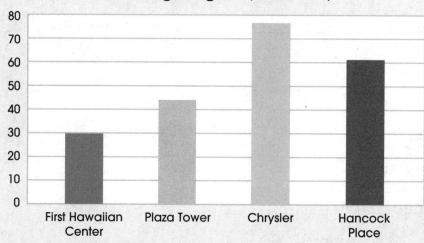

Building Heights (in stories)

1. Which is the tallest building? _____

2. Which building is about twice the height of First Hawaiian Center? _____

_____

3. The Empire State Building has 102 stories. Which building is about a third its

height? _____

Puzzler

This coordinate grid has 20 letters on it.

Write the ordered pairs to spell a word for each clue.

A flower:

_____

A kitchen appliance:

_____

A fruit:

_____

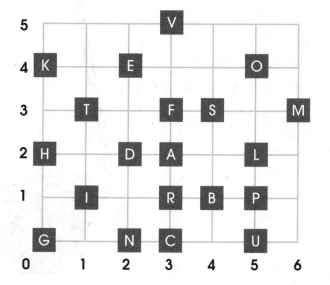

Reading & Math Practice, Grade 4 © 2014 Scholastic Inc.

WORD of the Day

Use the word below in a sentence about someone who has learned much by studying a subject.

scholar: (adj.) *person whose work is to do serious learning or research; expert in a field of study*

_____

_____

Sentence Mender

Rewrite the sentence to make it correct.

They should'nt play there music so lowd when kid's are trying to sleep?

_____

Cursive Quote

Copy the quotation in cursive writing.

Not all readers are leaders, but all leaders are readers.

—Harry S. Truman

Why does Truman advise leaders to read? Write your answer in cursive on another sheet of paper.

Analogy of the Day

Complete the analogy.

Tornado is to **damage** as _____ is to **fever**.

○ A. illness   ○ B. health   ○ C. hurricane   ○ D. fracture

Explain how the analogy works: _____

_____

Ready, Set, READ!

Read the passage. Then answer the questions.

A Mystery of Speed

Jack "Rabbit" Jones is a swift runner—as fast as lightning. As fast as an arrow. He can get to a pork chop faster than a dog can. He can keep up with a race car. When he plays baseball, he can pop the ball into the air and round the bases before the ball comes down. I know because I saw him do it.

But recently I heard a story about Rabbit that even I couldn't believe. Nina "The Nose" Ramirez saw it with her own eyes. She told me that she watched Rabbit enter his room, flick off the light switch by the door, and get into his bed before the room was dark.

Now I know Nina—she's accepts only the facts. And facts are only facts if she sees them with her own two peepers. What Rabbit did sounds impossible, even for him. How did he do it? I need to get back to Nina.

1. What are *peepers*?

   ○ A. spies   ○ B. eyes   ○ C. reporters   ○ D. binoculars

2. Believe it or not, Rabbit did just what Nina saw him do. How do you think he did it?

   Explain. _____

   _____

⊚ BrainTeaser ⊚

It's a festive summer street fair! What might you see? Write 26 different nouns. Use each letter from *a* to *z* to begin each word. The sentence is started for you.

At the street fair, I saw **a**rtists, **b**ands, **c**lowns, **d**_____

_____

_____

_____

Reading & Math Practice, Grade 4 © 2014 Scholastic Inc.

Number Place

Compare. Write **<**, **=**, or **>**.

2.5 _____ 0.5   1.5 _____ 1.8

3.7 _____ 7.3   39.4 _____ 39

60.7 _____ sixty-seven   9.6 _____ nine and six tenths

FAST Math

Find the missing numbers in the fact family patterns.

If $3 \times 50 = 150$, then $150 \div 3 =$ _____ .

If $6 \times 70 = 420$, then $420 \div 6 =$ _____ .

If $7 \times 40 =$ _____ , then _____ $\div 7 = 40$.

If $320 \div 8 = 40$, then $8 \times 40 =$ _____ .

If $540 \div 9 = 60$, then $9 \times 60 =$ _____ .

If $400 \div 4 =$ _____ , then $4 \times 100 =$ _____ .

Think Tank

The first modern Olympics was held in 1896. The winning time in the 100-meter dash was 12 seconds. In 2008 the winning time was 9.69 seconds. How much faster was the 2008 winning time?

_____

Show your work in the tank.

Data Place

The line plot shows students' science test scores. Use the data to answer the questions.

Science Test Scores

```
                                        X
                                        X
                                        X
                                X       X
                                X   X   X   X
                            X   X   X   X   X
            X               X   X   X   X   X   X
    0   5  10  15  20  25  30  35  40  45  50  55  60  65  70  75  80  85  90  95 100
```

1. How many students took the test? _____

2. What is the range of the data? _____

3. What is the mode of the data? _____

4. How many students scored lower than 80? _____

5. Which score is an outlier? _____ How do you know?

_____

Puzzler

Write the numbers 1,000, 2,000, 3,000, 4,000, and 5,000 *once* each in the five boxes. Make the sum of the three numbers in each direction total 10,000.

How did you solve the problem?

_____

_____

_____

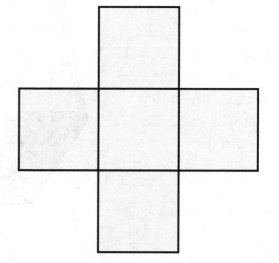

134

Reading & Math Practice, Grade 4 © 2014 Scholastic Inc.

WORD of the Day

Use the word below in a sentence about taking a relaxing day off.

carefree: (adj.) *without care or worries; happy; cheerful*

_____

_____

Sentence Mender

Rewrite the sentence to make it correct.

Stephen foster the grate American songwriter was born on july 4 1828.

_____

Cursive Quote

Copy the quotation in cursive writing.

No one is perfect. That's why pencils have erasers.

—Anonymous

_____

_____

_____

How can this saying cheer people up? Respond in cursive on another sheet of paper.

Analogy of the Day

Complete the analogy.

Teapot is to **brew** as _____ is to **bake**.

○ A. cake   ○ B. oven   ○ C. coffee   ○ D. turkey

Explain how the analogy works: _____

_____

Ready, Set, READ!

Read the passage. Then answer the questions.

"No Water, No Life"

Sylvia Earle is an ocean scientist, explorer, and teacher. She has spent over 7,000 hours under the sea. She set a record for the deepest solo dive. No wonder her friends call her "Your Deepness!"

Dr. Earle urges everyone to protect our oceans. She hopes her words will convince you because, as she says, "No blue, no green."

• *With every drop of water you drink, every breath you take, you're connected to the sea, no matter where on earth you live.*

• *People ask: Why should I care about the ocean? Because the ocean is the cornerstone of earth's life-support system. It shapes climate and weather. It holds most of life on earth. The ocean holds 97% of earth's water. It's the blue heart of the planet; we should take care of our heart. It's what makes life possible for us.*

• *I believe we should be taking care of the ocean as if our lives depend on it—because they do.*

1. Why are some words in *italics*?

_____

_____

_____

_____

_____

_____

2. Explain "No blue, no green" in your own words.

_____

_____

_____

_____

_____

_____

☙ BrainTeaser ☙

Imagine an adventure to anywhere at any time—past, present, or future! Write 26 different verbs for actions or feelings you **might have**. Use each letter from *a* to *z* to begin each word. The sentence is started for you.

On my adventure to _____ I might **a**dmire, **b**lush,

_____

_____

_____

Reading & Math Practice, Grade 4 © 2014 Scholastic Inc.

Number Place

Order the decimals from *least* to *greatest*.

1.6   1.2   1.9   1.5   _____

6.4   6.7   6.8   6.1   _____

Order the decimals from *greatest* to *least*.

10.1   10.9   0.4   10.6   _____

12.7   12.3   11.9   12.8   _____

FAST Math

Use number sense to estimate each quotient.

37 ÷ 8 = _____   34 ÷ 9 = _____   429 ÷ 7 = _____

624 ÷ 9 = _____   155 ÷ 4 = _____   650 ÷ 8 = _____

29 ÷ 4 = _____   428 ÷ 6 = _____   493 ÷ 5 = _____

Think Tank

How many seconds are there in 2 hours?

_____

Show your work in the tank.

Data Place

Students counted the number of cousins they have.

Finish the table. Then answer the questions below.

Number of Cousins

Range	Tallies	Number
0–4	||||| ||	
5–8		42
9–12	||||| ||||| ||||| |||||		
13–16	||||| ||||| ||||| ||	
17 or more		9

1. Which range has three times as many tallies as 0–4? _____

2. Which range has half as many tallies as 5–8? _____

3. Which range would include the number of cousins you have?

_____

Puzzler

Half a design appears on one side of a line of symmetry.
Complete the rest of the design. Keep it symmetrical.

138

WORD of the Day

Use the word below in a sentence about eating a big meal.

digest: (v.) *to process food inside the body to change it into a form the body can use*

_____

_____

Sentence Mender

Rewrite the sentence to make it correct.

May please I have you autograf prince william.

_____

Cursive Quote

Copy the quotation in cursive writing.

A journey of a thousand miles begins with one step.

—Lao-tzu

_____

_____

_____

_____

What can make taking a first step so hard? Write your answer in cursive on another sheet of paper.

Analogy of the Day

Complete the analogy.

Weak is to **mighty** as _____ is to **noisy**.

○ A. silent   ○ B. strong   ○ C. loud   ○ D. muscle

Explain how the analogy works: _____

_____

📖 Ready, Set, READ!

Read the poem.
Then answer the questions.

Swift Things Are Beautiful
by Elizabeth Coatsworth

Swift things are beautiful:
Swallows and deer,
And lightning that falls
Bright-veined and clear,
Rivers and meteors,
Wind in the wheat,
The strong-withered horse,
The runner's sure feet.

And slow things are beautiful:
The closing of day,
The pause of the wave
That curves downward to spray,
The ember that crumbles,
The opening flower,
And the ox that moves on
In the quiet of power.

1. What is another word for *ember*?
   ○ A. jewel   ○ C. flame
   ○ B. cinder   ○ D. cookie

2. What do the things in verse 1 have in common?

   _____

   _____

   _____

   In verse 2?

   _____

   _____

   _____

3. *Withers* are part of a horse's back. What does "strong-withered" mean?

   _____

   _____

   _____

🌀 BrainTeaser 🌀

The sentence in the box has only seven words.
But every word starts with the *same* letter.

Write a sentence in which every word begins with *h*.
Make it as long as you can.

> **C**lever **c**ousin **C**lark **c**heerfully
> **c**leans **c**rusty **c**arpets.

_____

_____

_____

_____

140

Reading & Math Practice, Grade 4 © 2014 Scholastic Inc.

Number Place

Compare. Write **<**, **=**, or **>**.

2.05 _____ 0.05   1.35 _____ 1.38

3.71 _____ 3.70   49.60 _____ 49.06

6.47 _____ sixty-four and seventy hundredths

three and eighteen hundredths _____ 3.18

FAST Math

Use number sense to estimate each quotient.

389 ÷ 8 = _____   314 ÷ 6 = _____   4,166 ÷ 7 = _____

173 ÷ 3 = _____   3,572 ÷ 4 = _____   3,177 ÷ 8 = _____

6,341 ÷ 9 = _____   2,439 ÷ 6 = _____   3,583 ÷ 5 = _____

Think Tank

A golfer hit a 250-yard shot and then a 130-yard shot to the hole. How many feet did she hit the ball, in total?

_____

Show your work in the tank.

Data Place

The table provides data on school populations.

Display the data in a bar graph. Give your graph a title and add the labels.

School	Populations
Chavez	976
McAuliffe	723
Rita Dove	1,020
Whitman	897

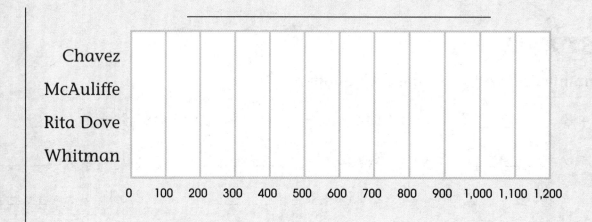

Write the school names in population order from largest to smallest.

_____

Puzzler

Try this toothpick challenge.
Rearrange the 12 toothpicks to
make 3 squares that are
congruent (the same size and shape).

Reading & Math Practice, Grade 4 © 2014 Scholastic Inc.

WORD of the Day

Use the word below in a sentence about an early family member you know about.

ancestor: (n.) *someone who came before you in your family, especially earlier than a grandparent*

_____

_____

Sentence Mender

Rewrite the sentence to make it correct.

Are sumer garden in full blum is as pritty as a pitcher.

_____

Cursive Quote

Copy the quotation in cursive writing.

Reading is to the mind what exercise is to the body.

—Joseph Addison

- -

_____

_____

Do you agree with this statement? Explain your view in cursive on another sheet of paper.

Analogy of the Day

Complete the analogy.

Interesting is to **fascinating** as _____ is to **spotless**.

○ A. dull   ○ B. filthy   ○ C. clean   ○ D. spotted

Explain how the analogy works: _____

_____

📖 Ready, Set, READ!

Read the passage. Then answer the questions.

Travel Essay: Following the Astronauts

I can't go to the moon, so I found a closer stand-in. It is Craters of the Moon National Monument in Idaho. The area was formed by volcanic activity hundreds of centuries ago. Burning lava destroyed its plants and animals. However, it left behind new landforms. Many exist nowhere else in the United States. Best of all, it looks like the moon.

I'm a travel writer, not a scientist. But Craters of the Moon really sparked my interest. I wanted to know why it was once a classroom for astronauts! Those pioneers were pilots, not rock experts. NASA scientists wanted them to learn about the rocks so they could know what to look for on the moon.

So the astronauts studied lava flows, rocks, and land features at Craters of the Moon. I did, too. Soon I began to spot differences among the many lava rocks. Park rangers challenged us to see things many visitors miss. I loved my whole trip. And I traveled by van, not by rocket!

1. Astronauts went to Craters of the Moon to
   - ○ A. travel by van
   - ○ B. study lava rocks
   - ○ C. increase strength
   - ○ D. relax before a flight

2. Which phrase best describes this national monument?
   - ○ A. Lunar-like landscape
   - ○ B. Family fun spot
   - ○ C. Rock heaven
   - ○ D. Science lab

🌀 BrainTeaser 🌀

Climb the word ladder to change *corn* to *husk*. Change only one letter at a time. Write the new word on each step.

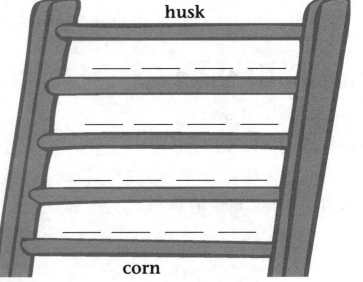

husk

corn

Reading & Math Practice, Grade 4 © 2014 Scholastic Inc.

Number Place

Order the decimals from *least* to *greatest*.

1.06   1.02   1.92   1.05   _____

6.43   6.73   4.47   6.14   _____

Order the decimals from *greatest* to *least*.

10.01   10.91   9.99   10.06   _____

12.37   11.23   10.16   12.23   _____

FAST Math

Find each quotient.

72 ÷ 3 = _____   48 ÷ 2 = _____   64 ÷ 4 = _____

98 ÷ 7 = _____   114 ÷ 3 = _____   126 ÷ 6 = _____

255 ÷ 5 = _____   176 ÷ 8 = _____   288 ÷ 9 = _____

💡 Think Tank

A punch recipe calls for 3 quarts of cranberry juice, 1 quart of orange juice, and 1 gallon of club soda. How many cups of cranberry juice does the recipe need?

_____

Show your work in the tank.

Data Place

The table shows the estimated populations of America's five largest cities, as of April 2010.

Use the table to answer the questions.

City	Population
New York, NY	8,175,133
Los Angeles, CA	3,792,621
Chicago, IL	2,695,598
Houston, TX	2,099,451
Philadelphia, PA	1,526,006

1. Which city's population rounds to 3,000,000?

   _____

2. Which two cities differ in population by about 1,700,000? _____

   _____

3. Which city has about 3 times as many people as Chicago?_____

   _____

4. Suppose Philadelphia's population increases by about 500,000. About how many

   people would live there? _____

Puzzler

Color the design.
Use the key.

If the decimal is	Color the space
> 1.0	blue
= 0.5	purple
< 0.5	green

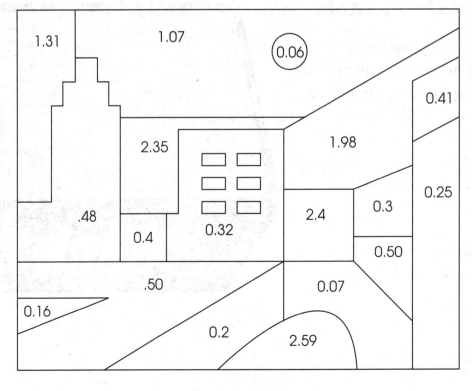

Reading & Math Practice, Grade 4 © 2014 Scholastic Inc.

WORD of the Day

Use the word below in a sentence about someone who is easy to trick.

gullible: (adj.) *too ready to believe what people say; easily cheated or tricked*

_____

_____

Sentence Mender

Rewrite the sentence to make it correct.

Lets put some beens cucumbers cheese beats in the salad.

_____

Cursive Quote

Copy the quotation in cursive writing.

Stories are like children. They grow in their own way.

—Madeleine L'Engel

_____

_____

_____

Do you agree with L'Engel that stories are like children? Explain in cursive on another sheet of paper.

Analogy of the Day

Complete the analogy.

Roof is to **house** as _____ is to **room**.

○ A. cabin   ○ B. ceiling   ○ C. kitchen   ○ D. chimney

Explain how the analogy works: _____

_____

Ready, Set, READ!

Read the tall tale. Then answer the questions.

Pecos Bill Rides a Tornado

Everybody in Kansas knew that Pecos Bill could ride anything that moved. No bull or bronco could throw him. Far's I know, Bill never even got thrown when he came here to ride a tornado.

Now Bill wouldn't ride just any tornado! He waited for the wildest twister Kansas ever had. It turned the sky green and black, and roared so loud it woke up half of China. Bill roped that tornado, wrestled it to the ground, and jumped upon its back. The tornado whipped and whirled and spun all the way to Texas. It tied rivers into knots and flattened forests as it went. Bill just hung on, whooping and hooting and sometimes jabbing it with his spurs.

That tornado was beat. So it headed to California to rain itself dry. It let go of so much water on the way that it carved out the Grand Canyon. It was down to near nothing when Bill got off to grab a nap. The tornado hit the ground so hard it sank below sea level. Folks call that spot Death Valley.

1. List three facts hidden in this tall tale.

1) _____
_____
_____

2) _____
_____
_____

3) _____
_____
_____

2. Which real sport has bulls and broncos?
- A. car racing
- B. horse racing
- C. hockey
- D. rodeo

BrainTeaser

What does each saying mean? Read the definitions on the right.
Write the number on the line.

1. I **kept my chin up**.   _____ harder than one can manage

2. Let's not **split hairs**.   _____ what you'd normally expect

3. I'm **in over my head**.   _____ shows no shock or surprise

4. What an **eager beaver**!   _____ argue every little detail

5. She **threw in the towel**.   _____ didn't lose hope

6. He didn't **bat an eyelash**.   _____ hard worker

7. That's **par for the course**.   _____ gave up

148

Reading & Math Practice, Grade 4 © 2014 Scholastic Inc.

Number Place

Finish labeling the number line to show equivalent decimals and fractions.

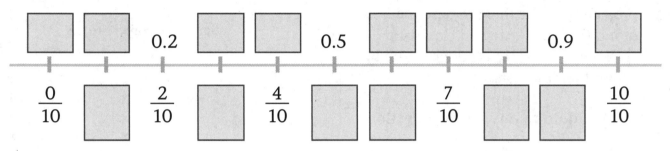

FAST Math

Find each quotient.

$9\overline{)681}$ $5\overline{)265}$ $8\overline{)352}$ $9\overline{)301}$

$4\overline{)74}$ $2\overline{)29}$ $6\overline{)124}$ $3\overline{)418}$

Think Tank

Luz played soccer for $2\frac{3}{4}$ hours on Monday and for $1\frac{1}{4}$ hours on Tuesday. How much longer did Luz play on Monday?

_____

Show your work in the tank.

Data Place

Mr. Bunsen's students are working on science projects. He asks them to describe how far along they are. "Are you closest to $\frac{1}{4}$ done, $\frac{1}{2}$ done, $\frac{3}{4}$ done, or all done?" The line plot shows their answers.

Use the data to answer the questions.

1. How many students are in the class?

   _____

2. What is the range of the data?

   _____

3. What is the answer that came up most often?

   _____

4. How many students are at least half done? _____

   What fraction of the class is that? _____

Science Project Status

```
                      X
                      X
                      X
              X       X
              X       X
              X       X
              X       X
              X       X
      X       X       X
      X       X       X
      X       X       X
      X       X       X       X
     ───────────────────────────
      1       1       3
      ─       ─       ─       1
      4       2       4
```

Puzzler

Greene Farm has a total of 36 goats and geese. Farmer Greene reports that there are 100 legs in all.

How many of each animal are on the farm?

_____ geese

_____ goats

WORD
of the Day

Use the word below in a sentence about how to get new members for a club or team.

recruit: (v.) *to get people to join or become new members*

_____

_____

Sentence Mender

Rewrite the sentence to make it correct.

Who winter cote have lost it's hood.

_____

Cursive Quote

Copy the quotation in cursive writing.

A single arrow is easily broken, but not ten in a bundle.

—Japanese proverb

_____

_____

_____

_____

Does this proverb make sense to you? Why? Write your explanation in cursive on another sheet of paper.

Analogy of the Day

Complete the analogy.

Yolk is to **egg** as _____ is to **recipe**.

○ A. shell   ○ B. cook   ○ C. ingredient   ○ D. eat

Explain how the analogy works: _____

_____

📖 Ready, Set, READ!

Read the passage. Then answer the questions.

Heavenly Hats

Anthony Leanna got a big idea when he was ten years old. He was visiting his sick grandmother in the hospital. There he saw people who had lost all their hair. It had fallen out because of disease and the medicine they took to help them get well. "I knew that if I was in the hospital and had lost my hair, I would want a hat to wear," he said.

So Anthony started a project. He called it Heavenly Hats. He collected hats to give to patients who needed them. Why did he do this? He says that he wanted to help "people who were going through a very tough time."

Heavenly Hats began in 2001. Since then it has given away over a million hats! You can learn more about Anthony and his project online.

1. How can a hat cheer someone up? _____

_____

2. How does the writer of this piece help you understand Anthony's ideas?

_____

🌀 BrainTeaser 🌀

What do sea monsters eat?

Solve each clue. Then copy each letter into its numbered box to find the answer to the riddle.

- Discovers or locates

  $\overline{}_{1}$ $\overline{}_{10}$ $\overline{}_{6}$ $\overline{}_{7}$ $\overline{}_{8}$

- Belt made of ribbon

  $\overline{}_{12}$ $\overline{}_{5}$ $\overline{}_{3}$ $\overline{}_{9}$

- Part between waist and thigh

  $\overline{}_{4}$ $\overline{}_{2}$ $\overline{}_{11}$

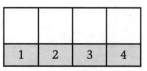
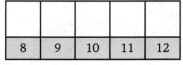

1	2	3	4

5	6	7

8	9	10	11	12

Reading & Math Practice: Grade 4 © 2014 Scholastic Inc.

Number Place

Make a 4-digit decimal place value chart from tens to hundredths. Label the columns. Then write the following decimals in number form in your chart:

- fourteen and fifty-nine hundredths
- twenty and six hundredths

FAST Math

Find each quotient.

$720 \div 4 =$ _____ $624 \div 3 =$ _____ $2,900 \div 2 =$ _____

$601 \div 7 =$ _____ $1,024 \div 6 =$ _____ $3,262 \div 5 =$ _____

Think Tank

Krin danced for 30 minutes every morning and for 45 minutes every afternoon for 5 days. How many hours and minutes did he dance in all?

_____

Show your work in the tank.

Data Place

Use the data in the calendar to answer the questions.

APRIL

SUN	MON	TUE	WED	THU	FRI	SAT
			1	2	3	4
5	6	7	8	9	10	11
12	13	14	15	16	17	18
19	20	21	22	23	24	25
26	27	28	29	30		

1. Four dates in a row have a sum of 74. What are the dates?

   _____

2. Two dates in a row have a product of 240. What are the dates?

   _____

3. Which two dates have a quotient of 3 and a sum of 32? _____

4. Which two dates have product of 108 and a difference of 3? _____

Puzzler

When the power stops, so do the electric clocks. Solve the word problems.

1. The clock says _____ .

   The power has been back on for 7 minutes.

   It was off for 52 minutes.

   The correct time should be _____ .

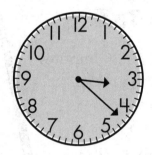

2. This clock says _____ .

   The power has been back on since 11:45.

   It was off for 35 minutes.

   The correct time should be _____ .

WORD of the Day

Use the word below in a sentence about a smart safety plan.

policy: (n.) *a plan, rule, or way of acting; program*

_____

_____

Sentence Mender

Rewrite the sentence to make it correct.

Witch one of these knew song did you liked the less?

_____

Cursive Quote

Copy the quotation in cursive writing.

Always laugh when you can. It is cheap medicine.

—Lord Byron

- -

- -

- -

- -

Do you agree with Byron's advice? Write your answer in cursive on another sheet of paper.

Analogy of the Day

Complete the analogy.

Hiker is to **hiking** as _____ is to **entertaining**.

○ A. walking   ○ B. laughing   ○ C. mountain   ○ D. clown

Explain how the analogy works: _____

_____

Ready, Set, READ!

Read the journal entry.
Then answer the questions.

4 June, 1498

　We've now been four weeks on the rolling sea. Life aboard the *Mathew* is demanding. It's my first voyage as a ship's boy. I sleep below deck wrapped in part of an old sail. Colin sleeps beside me, but we don't have bunks. It's uncomfortable, and so cramped that we can't stand up straight.

　I am but eleven years old, yet my job is better than Colin's. He's a swabber who mops all day to clean the decks. I flip the ship's half-hour glass. It's our only timepiece, so I've been most diligent at my job. Still, we avoid Mr. Stone, the cruel bosun. He's a short-tempered fellow, always ready to snap his cat-o'-nine-tails hard across our tender young hides.

　When free, I keep mainly to myself. At times, a friendly seaman will teach me to tie knots, or to splice, wind, and tie the deck ropes. I must learn as much as I can if I hope to become a captain's servant on my next voyage.

1. What is a cat-o'-nine-tails?
   ○ A. a pet
   ○ B. a sail
   ○ C. a whip
   ○ D. an oar

2. Why would the boy hope to become a captain's servant?

_____

_____

_____

_____

_____

_____

_____

_____

⑨ BrainTeaser ⑥

How many different words can you spell with letters from the word *denominators*?
Every word must have at least three letters. List them here.

_____

_____

_____

_____

_____

Reading & Math Practice, Grade 4 © 2014 Scholastic Inc.

Number Place

Compare. Write **<**, **=**, or **>**.

2.5 _____ 0.25

0.7 _____ 0.07

50.7 _____ fifty-seven

1.5 _____ 1.08

9.02 _____ nine and two tenths

0.4 _____ 40

FAST Math

Find each quotient.

3,200 ÷ 4 = _____

6,015 ÷ 7 = _____

6,024 ÷ 3 = _____

1,024 ÷ 5 = _____

2,907 ÷ 2 = _____

3,268 ÷ 6 = _____

Think Tank

Greg does sit-ups every day. On 4 of the past 5 days he did 50, 60, 40, and 80 sit-ups. His average was 60 sit-ups a day over the 5 days. So how many sit-ups did he do on the fifth day?

_____

Show your work in the tank.

Data Place

All the students at Gershwin School were asked to name their favorite music group. The results for the top five answers are shown.

Use the data in the table to answer the questions.

Music Group	Votes
Hot Potatoes	203
The Mangoes	142
The Bugs	108
Louder Still	71
Popped Corn	36

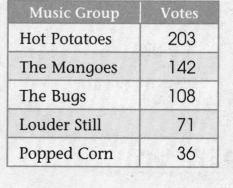

1. How many votes did these groups get altogether? _____

2. Which group got about $\frac{1}{4}$ of the votes?

   _____

3. Which group got $\frac{1}{3}$ the number of votes The Bugs got?

   _____

4. Which group got half as many votes as the Mangoes got?

   _____

Puzzler

Shade a picture in each grid. Draw anything you like— but make its area match the amounts shown.

0.34 + 0.3

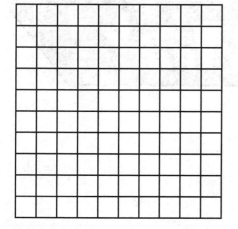

0.78 – 0.43

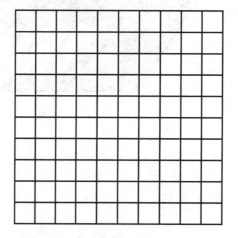

WORD of the Day

Use the word below in a sentence about a rude remark.

flippant: (adj.) *lacking respect or seriousness; rude; jokey*

_____

_____

Sentence Mender

Rewrite the sentence to make it correct.

Its total impossable to keep your eyes open when you sneezed

_____

Cursive Quote

Copy the quotation in cursive writing.

No act of kindness, no matter how small, is ever wasted.

—Aesop

- -

- -

- -

How can a small kind act make a lasting impression? Write your answer in cursive on another sheet of paper.

Analogy of the Day

Complete the analogy.

Glass is to **shattered** as _____ is to **torn**.

○ A. cry   ○ B. brick   ○ C. paper   ○ D. window

Explain how the analogy works: _____

_____

Ready, Set, READ!

Read the passage. Then answer the questions.

Burying the Hatchet

Have you ever heard the expression "Let's bury the hatchet?" A hatchet is an axe. The expression refers to an old custom that some Native American groups used to end war and make peace.

Chiefs decided when to stop fighting. They held a ceremony together. Each offered to bury his own hatchet to "seal the deal." They might pick a spot beneath a tree or in a riverbed. This gesture was an act of trust, like shaking hands. It showed that both chiefs were willing to put aside their differences and move on.

The expression "to bury the hatchet" means to forget about disagreements and be friends again. Suppose two brothers who want a pet aren't getting along. They might agree to "bury the hatchet" to make a point to their parents. It would show that they are finally ready to cooperate for the pet.

1. Why would both chiefs give their hatchets for the peace ceremony?

_____

_____

2. How does the author explain the meaning of this expression?

_____

_____

⏺ BrainTeaser ⏺

Solve the puzzle.

It has a two-letter word on top and an eight-letter word at the bottom. Going down, each word uses the same letters as the word above it, plus one more, and then rearranged.

Clues:
• On, by, or near
• Had food
• Group of soccer players
• Tried to explain
• Related to the mind
• Shelves over a fireplace
• Medical problems

160

Reading & Math Practice, Grade 4 © 2014 Scholastic Inc.

Number Place

Order the decimals from *least* to *greatest*.

0.42	0.09	0.35	_____
0.63	0.2	0.43	_____
0.4	0.04	0.38	_____
0.75	0.57	0.06	_____

FAST Math

Write a fraction for the shaded part. Circle any fraction that shows less than one half.

_____   _____   _____   _____

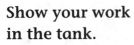 **Think Tank**

Jeb hikes Grand Canyon trails. He hiked 1.7 miles on North Kaibab, 4.9 miles on Bright Angel, and 4.4 miles on South Kaibab. What is the difference in length between his longest and shortest hikes?

_____

Show your work in the tank.

Data Place

Use the train schedule to answer the questions below.

Leaves	Time	Arrives	Time
Tulip	10:00 A.M.	Rose	10:25 A.M.
Rose	10:29 A.M.	Lilac	10:44 A.M.
Lilac	10:48 A.M.	Crocus	11:26 A.M.
Crocus	11:30 A.M.	Aster	12:15 P.M.

1. Which is the shortest trip? _____

2. Which trip lasts 38 minutes? _____

3. At what time do you think the train arrives at Tulip? _____

4. When do you think the train leaves Aster? _____

Puzzler

Fill in this design using 4 different colors. You can repeat colors—but not where sections touch.

162

WORD of the Day

Use the word below in a sentence to tell what "raised eyebrows" might mean.

indicate: (v.) *to show, prove, or point out clearly; specify*

_____

_____

Sentence Mender

Rewrite the sentence to make it correct.

A ostriches eye is bigger then it's brain!

_____

Cursive Quote

Copy the quotation in cursive writing.

Any kid will run any errand for you if you ask at bedtime.

—Red Skelton

_____

_____

_____

Do you think that Skelton is correct? Explain your views in cursive on another sheet of paper.

Analogy of the Day

Complete the analogy.

Relax is to **tighten** as _____ is to **fail**.

○ A. loose   ○ B. rest   ○ C. flunk   ○ D. pass

Explain how the analogy works: _____

_____

📖 Ready, Set, READ!

Read the myth. Then answer the questions.

Jaguar, Master of Fire   A *Myth From South America*

In ancient days, humans of the jungle were weak creatures. They had no weapons. Finding enough food to eat was a daily struggle. If they caught an animal, they had to eat it raw because they did not yet have fire.

Jaguar was stronger and wiser. This sleek cat had powerful legs, keen ears and eyes, and sharp teeth. His bows and arrows made him an expert hunter. Jaguar, Master of Fire, cooked his meat.

Jaguar was kind then. He pitied the humans. One day Jaguar came upon a starving man. He gently led the weak man to his den. Jaguar showed him fire. Jaguar grilled meat to feed the man, who ate with ravenous pleasure. Jaguar showed his weapons and taught the man to hunt with them.

The man owed his life to Jaguar. But he realized that Jaguar had given him new power. Alas, the man repaid Jaguar's kindness with cruelty. He killed Jaguar's wife and stole his fire. Since then, humans and jaguars have feared each other. Humans know that jaguars wait to take revenge on them.

1. What made Jaguar stronger and wiser than ancient humans? _____

_____

2. How did Jaguar's encounter with the man change both of them? _____

_____

🌀 BrainTeaser 🌀

The word bank lists astronomy words.
Each word is hidden in the puzzle.
Find and circle each word.

Word Bank

ASTEROID	GALAXY	PLANET
COMET	METEOR	SATELLITE
CORONA	MILKY WAY	SOLAR
ECLIPSE	NEBULA	SOLSTICE
EQUINOX	ORBIT	STAR
FLARES	PHASE	SUNSPOTS

```
E M G C E W B K R O E T E M
C I S E O S I F G A L A X Y
I L V O L M A Z P C T S O B
T K S S Q E E H V H W S Y R
S Y U S L T K T P Z Z T S B
L W N D W I D I O R E T S A
O A S M G L J I B N O E X S
S Y P N S L L B A R C O E C
L H O E O E H L B L N R Y O
I K T B L T P I I I A X W R
X A S U A A T P U L A H X O
X V P L R S S Q F L O B X N
A T S A M E E B A L B D I A
```

Reading & Math Practice, Grade 4 © 2014 Scholastic Inc.

Number Place

Write the decimal from the balloon that fits
each clue. One number is *not* used.

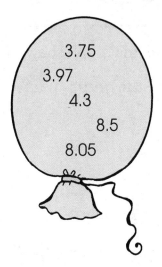

3.75
3.97
4.3
8.5
8.05

_____ is much nearer to 8 than to 9.

_____ is halfway between 8 and 9.

_____ is the same as three and three fourths.

_____ is a little less than 4.

FAST Math

Write a mixed number for the shaded area of each picture.

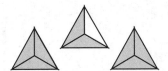 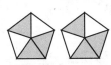  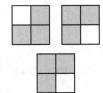

_____   _____   _____   _____

Think Tank

Renee spent $18.95 on a
scarf, $39.95 on sweater,
and $19.79 on a hat.
About how much change
should she get if she pays
with a $100 bill?

_____

Show your work
in the tank.

Data Place

The line graph shows attendance at a new museum.

Use the graph to answer the questions.

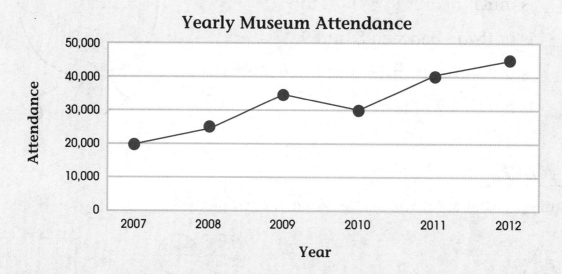

Yearly Museum Attendance

1. How many people visited the museum in 2007? _____

2. How many more visitors were there in 2011 than in 2010? _____

3. How many people visited the museum from 2010 to 2012? _____

4. What can you say about museum attendance over the six years? _____

_____

Puzzler

Write 2 times when the clock hands would form:

• a right angle   _____

• a 180° angle   _____

• an obtuse angle   _____

• an acute angle   _____

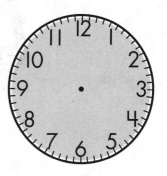

Reading & Math Practice, Grade 4 © 2014 Scholastic Inc.

WORD of the Day

Use the word below in a sentence about a school volunteer.

volunteer: (n.) *a person who works without pay; someone who offers help, advice, or service by choice*

_____

_____

Sentence Mender

Rewrite the sentence to make it correct.

The worlds heavyest onion wayed more than a mans head!

_____

Cursive Quote

Copy the quotation in cursive writing.

We can learn something new any time we believe we can.

—Virginia Satir

_____

_____

_____

How can believing lead to success? Write your answer in cursive on another sheet of paper.

Analogy of the Day

Complete the analogy.

Nickel is to **coin** as _____ is to **tool**.

○ A. wrench   ○ B. dime   ○ C. bill   ○ D. plumber

Explain how the analogy works: _____

_____

Ready, Set, READ!

Read the book review. Then answer the questions.

A Review of *Peter and the Starcatchers*

Peter and the Starcatchers is a novel by Dave Barry and Ridley Pearson. It explains how Peter Pan came to be. It's a long book, but I loved it. I even let my parents borrow it!

This book has many parts that would be familiar to readers who know the original Peter Pan story. You meet orphans, pirates, mermaids, and a crocodile. There is a shipwreck, some stardust, many secrets, and dashing swordfights. Black Stache is the pirate who later becomes Captain Hook. The authors made up some new characters, too, such as Molly. She tries to keep the stardust away from the pirates. She also helps Peter become the character originally created over a century ago.

This book switches moods a lot. It is wild, silly, playful, scary, and sad. What I liked best is that it mixed goofy humor with old-fashioned story-telling. I bet it would make a great read-aloud—if you have lots of time!

1. A sequel is a later installment of a story. This book is a *prequel*. How would you explain what a prequel is? _____

   _____

2. The reviewer liked the many mood switches in this book. How can mood switches keep a reader interested? _____

   _____

◉ BrainTeaser ◉

Each sentence below has two blanks. Both use the same letters to form different three-letter words. Fill them in.

1. Only two of the _____ boys can reach the top of the _____.

2. Use this soothing _____ for the cut on your _____.

3. There is a bear's _____ at the _____ of that path.

4. Soldiers in _____ may have to eat _____ food.

5. Is it okay for _____ to _____ your phone?

6. _____ that you _____ the bike, you can paint it pink.

168

Number Place

Order the decimals from *greatest* to *least*.

3.12	3.49	3.35	_____
8.63	8.2	8.49	_____
7.4	7.43	7.04	_____
20.75	20.07	20.7	_____

FAST Math

Write each fraction as the sum of unit fractions.

$\frac{3}{5}$ = _____

$\frac{3}{8}$ = _____

$\frac{7}{8}$ = _____

$\frac{4}{7}$ = _____

$\frac{5}{9}$ = _____

$\frac{8}{11}$ = _____

Think Tank

Juan scored an average of 22 points per game for his first 12 games. He scored 18 points per game in the next 12 games. How many points did he score in the first dozen games he played?

_____

Show your work in the tank.

Data Place

Use the table below to tally all vowels in the riddle and in its answer.

Why is a giraffe's neck so long?

Because its head is so far from its body!

Vowel	Tally	Number
a		
e		
i		
o		
u		
y		

Puzzler

Write the weights you would use.

1 kg $\frac{1}{2}$ kg 750 g 50 g 225 g

Total Weight	Weights Used
975 grams	
1,800 grams	
2,300 grams	

Reading & Math Practice, Grade 4 © 2014 Scholastic Inc.

WORD of the Day

Use the word below in a sentence about a foolish choice.

misguided: (adj.) *led to make mistakes or do wrong; foolish*

_____

_____

Sentence Mender

Rewrite the sentence to make it correct.

Each tiger have unique strips almost like people has fingerprince.

_____

Cursive Quote

Copy the quotation in cursive writing.

It's nice to be important, but it's more important to be nice.

—Author unknown

- -

- -

- -

- -

Explain what this saying means to you. Write your answer in cursive on another sheet of paper.

Analogy of the Day

Complete the analogy.

Spatula is to **cook** as _____ is to **archer**.

○ A. knife   ○ B. bow   ○ C. athlete   ○ D. medal

Explain how the analogy works: _____

_____

📖 Ready, Set, READ!

Read the passage. Then answer the questions.

Henna Body Art

Mehndi (MEN-dee) is the ancient art of body painting. It has been used in India and the Middle East for centuries. Mehndi designs look like tattoos, but they aren't. Designs are painted onto the skin.

First the artist prepares Mehndi "ink." This is done by crushing the leaves of the henna plant. The artist grinds them into powder, and then mixes in oils and other liquids to form a dark green paste.

Then the artist uses brushes or squeeze tubes to draw the design right onto the skin. It takes hours for large or detailed designs. After the design is done, the artist coats it with sugary lemon juice. This helps the design dry without smudging.

The next day, the wearer scrapes the paste off. By now, the henna has stained the skin and has turned from dark green to red-orange. By the day after, the mehndi turns brown. It can stay on for two or three weeks.

1. How would you describe the structure of the passage about mehndi?
   - ○ A. cause/effect
   - ○ B. question/answer
   - ○ C. time order
   - ○ D. problem/solution

2. How are mehndi and tattoos alike? _____

   _____

   _____

   _____

   How are they different?

   _____

   _____

   _____

   _____

⑨ BrainTeaser ⑥

Use the clues to complete each word that includes *j*.

1. Slightly open, like a door   ___ J ___ ___

2. An American form of music   J ___ ___ ___

3. Pop out of the DVD player   ___ J ___ ___ ___

4. Opposite of minor   ___ ___ J ___ ___

5. Stringed instrument   ___ ___ ___ J ___

6. Take pleasure in   ___ ___ J ___ ___

7. Thing or item   ___ ___ J ___ ___ ___

Reading & Math Practice, Grade 4 © 2014 Scholastic Inc.

Number Place

Round each decimal to the nearest tenth *and* hundredth.

Number	Nearest tenth	Nearest hundredth
6.177		
1.852		
4.335		

FAST Math

Write the value of *n* to complete the equivalent fraction.

$\dfrac{1}{2} = \dfrac{n}{6}$ _____ $\qquad$ $\dfrac{1}{4} = \dfrac{n}{8}$ _____ $\qquad$ $\dfrac{2}{5} = \dfrac{n}{10}$ _____ $\qquad$ $\dfrac{3}{8} = \dfrac{n}{16}$ _____

$\dfrac{4}{8} = \dfrac{n}{4}$ _____ $\qquad$ $\dfrac{2}{3} = \dfrac{n}{6}$ _____ $\qquad$ $\dfrac{6}{10} = \dfrac{n}{5}$ _____ $\qquad$ $\dfrac{5}{6} = \dfrac{n}{12}$ _____

$\dfrac{3}{9} = \dfrac{n}{3}$ _____ $\qquad$ $\dfrac{3}{4} = \dfrac{n}{8}$ _____ $\qquad$ $\dfrac{3}{4} = \dfrac{n}{12}$ _____ $\qquad$ $\dfrac{7}{8} = \dfrac{n}{24}$ _____

Think Tank

Look at the fruit market signs.

Which market has the better buy on pears?

_____

How much better?

_____

Show your work in the tank.

Fred's Fruit Market
Pears . . . . 3 for $.96
Apples . . . . 4 for $1

Fran's Fruit Market
Pears . . . . 6 for $1.80
Apples . . . . 2 for $.45

Data Place

Li tallied the kinds of vehicles that passed her house for 1 hour. Show her results in a line plot. Give the line plot a title.

Vehicle	Tally
Car	卌 IIII
Truck	II
Van	卌
SUV	卌 I
Bus	II

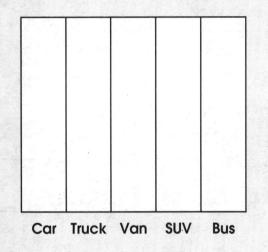

Car   Truck   Van   SUV   Bus

Summarize what the line plot shows.

_____

_____

_____

Puzzler

Use the fractions below to label the coins in each box. Then find each total value.

$\dfrac{4}{5}$ are dimes, $\dfrac{1}{5}$ are quarters.

$\dfrac{2}{3}$ are nickels, $\dfrac{1}{3}$ are quarters.

Total value: _____

Total value: _____

WORD of the Day

Use the word below in a sentence about why you might rest your feet on a stool or pillow.

elevate: (v.) *to raise or lift up*

_____

_____

Sentence Mender

Rewrite the sentence to make it correct.

Yesterday she was two sick to go to school but today he be better.

_____

Cursive Quote

Copy the quotation in cursive writing.

Never look down on anybody unless you're helping him up.

—Jesse Jackson

- -

- -

- -

What does Jackson mean to "look down on" someone? Write your answer in cursive on another sheet of paper.

Analogy of the Day

Complete the analogy.

Trunk is to **elephant** as _____ is to **fish**.

○ A. hook   ○ B. ocean   ○ C. gill   ○ D. tank

Explain how the analogy works: _____

_____

📖 Ready, Set, READ!

Read the passage. Then answer the questions.

The Hindu New Year

People everywhere mark special events with candles, lamps, or other lights. Diwali is the Hindu New Year. The word *Diwali* means "row of lamps." People light the Diwali lamps to welcome Lord Rama. They honor his victory over evil spirits. The lamps also help Lakshmi, the goddess of wealth, to find each home.

Diwali comes each fall. It lasts for three to five days, depending on local customs. *Diya* are small lamps used at Diwali. They are small bowls that hold oil. A cotton wick burns in the oil. People set diya all around their homes.

These are typical plans for the five days of Diwali.

• Day 1: Families get excited and ready. They clean, shop, and cook.

• Day 2: The diya are lit. Fireworks keep away evil spirits.

• Day 3: This is the main day of Diwali. There are many festive events.

• Day 4: This is the time for feasting and fun!

• Day 5: On this day, brothers and sisters honor their family bonds.

1. At what time of year do people celebrate Diwali?

○ A. winter   ○ B. spring   ○ C. summer   ○ D. autumn

2. What is the purpose of the list? _____

_____

🌀 BrainTeaser 🌀

Write the name of your favorite celebrity. Write 26 different adjectives to describe that person. Use each letter from *a* to *z* to begin each word. The sentence is started for you.

My favorite celebrity is _____ because he or she is

_____

_____

_____

_____

Reading & Math Practice, Grade 4 © 2014 Scholastic Inc.

Number Place

Write a decimal equal to each fraction.

$\frac{2}{5}$ _____ $\frac{2}{8}$ _____ $1\frac{1}{2}$ _____

$3\frac{9}{10}$ _____ $2\frac{6}{8}$ _____ $1\frac{3}{4}$ _____

$7\frac{1}{4}$ _____ $\frac{7}{10}$ _____ $5\frac{4}{5}$ _____

FAST Math ▶

Find the sum or difference in simplest form.

$\frac{7}{8} - \frac{3}{8} =$ _____ $\frac{9}{12} - \frac{5}{12} =$ _____ $\frac{1}{7} + \frac{5}{7} =$ _____

$\frac{7}{10} - \frac{4}{10} =$ _____ $\frac{1}{9} + \frac{4}{9} =$ _____ $\frac{8}{11} - \frac{2}{11} =$ _____

$\begin{array}{r} \frac{2}{6} \\ + \ \frac{4}{6} \\ \hline \end{array}$ $\begin{array}{r} \frac{2}{5} \\ + \ \frac{4}{5} \\ \hline \end{array}$ $\begin{array}{r} \frac{7}{8} \\ - \ \frac{2}{8} \\ \hline \end{array}$ $\begin{array}{r} \frac{9}{10} \\ - \ \frac{7}{10} \\ \hline \end{array}$

💡 Think Tank

At 6:00 A.M. the temperature was 45°F. It rose 13°F by noon. What was the temperature at noon?

_____

Show your work in the tank.

Data Place

Use the Venn diagram and numbers between 0 and 50. Write multiples of 4 in one part. Write multiples of 6 in the other part, and multiples of 4 and 6 in the overlapping part.

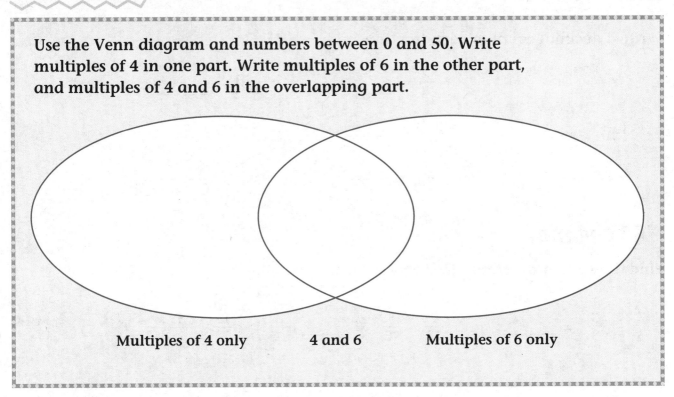

Multiples of 4 only   4 and 6   Multiples of 6 only

Puzzler

Find each small array inside the big array on the right. When you find it, circle it and write its number.

1   2   3

178

WORD of the Day

Use the word below in a sentence about a smart study plan.

strategy: (n.) *clever plan or system; skillful approach*

_____

_____

Sentence Mender

Rewrite the sentence to make it correct.

Yes jared prattice his piano lessin for fivteen minits a day

_____

Cursive Quote

Copy the quotation in cursive writing.

When you're thirsty it's too late to think about digging a well.

—Japanese proverb

. . . .

. . . .

. . . .

_____

What is another way to express this same idea? Write your answer in cursive on another sheet of paper.

Analogy of the Day

Complete the analogy.

Honey is to **sticky** as _____ is to **warm**.

○ A. ice   ○ B. soup   ○ C. freezer   ○ D. river

Explain how the analogy works: _____

_____

📖 Ready, Set, READ!

Read the story. Then answer the questions.

Mysti hadn't slept well. A series of crazy dreams kept her tossing and turning all night. By 4:45 A.M., she gave up and decided to read. She reached out to switch on her bedside lamp but recoiled in shock. She opened her mouth to scream, but no sound came out. Something was terribly wrong.

Mysti's long arms were now stumpy and scaly. She saw three long claws where her fingers should have been. Her eyesight, usually so sharp, was blurry. She headed to the mirror. But instead of walking across the room, Mysti found herself scuttling along on all fours, low to the ground. A bony tail trailed behind her.

Mysti had turned into an armadillo! Her tank-like body was covered with jointed, armor-like plates that made it hard to move. She desperately hoped that she was still dreaming. If not, this was going to be a difficult day . . .

1. What was Mysti's first clue that something was very wrong?
   - ○ A. She had a tail.
   - ○ B. She had bad dreams.
   - ○ C. Her vision was weak.
   - ○ D. She had scales and claws.

2. Another word that means the same as *scuttling* is
   - ○ A. hopping
   - ○ B. limping
   - ○ C. scampering
   - ○ D. slithering

ම BrainTeaser ෆ

What does each saying mean? Read the definitions on the right.
Write the number on the line.

1. I'm **in hot water** now.   _____ Good can come even from bad.

2. They are **going bananas!**   _____ What else would you expect?

3. He's the **apple of my eye**.   _____ acting emotional, wild, crazy

4. You **have a heart of gold**.   _____ the one I love most dearly

5. **Look for the silver lining**.   _____ are kind, caring, honest

6. It's time to **crack the books!**   _____ expecting big trouble

7. That's **how the cookie crumbles**.   _____ study hard

Reading & Math Practice, Grade 4 © 2014 Scholastic Inc.

Number Place

Write a fraction equal to each decimal.

0.35 _____   4.6 _____   3.75 _____   0.17 _____

5.97 _____   4.63 _____   0.85 _____   60.5 _____

FAST Math

Find the sum in simplest form.

$$6\frac{2}{6}$$
$$+\ 7\frac{4}{6}$$
———————

$$4\frac{2}{5}$$
$$+\ 1\frac{4}{5}$$
———————

$$3\frac{1}{3}$$
$$+\ 4\frac{1}{3}$$
———————

$$1\frac{3}{8}$$
$$+\ 7\frac{5}{8}$$
———————

$$6$$
$$+\ 3\frac{4}{9}$$
———————

$$2\frac{2}{8}$$
$$+\ 5\frac{4}{8}$$
———————

$$3\frac{1}{5}$$
$$+\ 8\frac{3}{5}$$
———————

$$2\frac{2}{4}$$
$$+\ 2\frac{3}{4}$$
———————

Think Tank

Find the area of the figure.

Area = _____ square units

Show your work
in the tank.

Data Place

What if dogs could vote? The graph shows how 60 dogs might vote if asked what kind of food they'd like for dinner.

Use the graph to answer the questions.

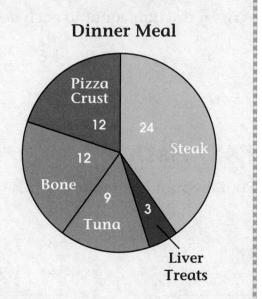

Dinner Meal

1. How many dogs chose pizza crust? _____

2. What food did $\frac{24}{60}$ of the dogs choose?

   _____

3. What food did 9 of the dogs choose?

   _____

4. What fraction of dogs did *not* choose steak or tuna? _____

5. Suppose 120 dogs voted. How many might a choose bone? _____

Puzzler

Write a letter from the code to make each number sentence true.

A = 1	B = 2	C = 3	D = 4	E = 5	F = 6	G = 7
H = 8	I = 9	J = 10	K = 11	L = 12	M = 13	N = 14
O = 15	P = 16	Q = 17	R = 18	S = 19	T = 20	U = 21
V = 22	W = 23	X = 24	Y = 25	Z = 26		

1. $C \times \underline{\hspace{1cm}} = X$

2. $Y \div E = \underline{\hspace{1cm}}$

3. $Y - Q = F + \underline{\hspace{1cm}}$

4. $J + T = C \times \underline{\hspace{1cm}}$

5. $\underline{\hspace{1cm}} - R = H \div A$

6. $U \div \underline{\hspace{1cm}} = C \times A$

7. $F \times \underline{\hspace{1cm}} = H \times I$

8. $C \times B + \underline{\hspace{1cm}} = K$

182

WORD of the Day

Use the word below in a sentence about learning a new dance.

awkward: (adj.) *clumsy; without grace or skill; embarrassing*

_____

_____

Sentence Mender

Rewrite the sentence to make it correct.

She's truely faverit athalete is socker player david beckham.

_____

Cursive Quote

Copy the quotation in cursive writing.

Don't let what you can't do stop you from what you can do.

—John Wooden

_____

_____

_____

_____

John Wooden was a great basketball coach. How might his statement inspire people on or off the basketball court? Write your answer in cursive on another sheet of paper.

Analogy of the Day

Complete the analogy.

Find is to **discover** as _____ is to **watch**.

○ A. wrist   ○ B. avoid   ○ C. lose   ○ D. view

Explain how the analogy works: _____

_____

📖 Ready, Set, READ!

Read the passage. Then answer the questions.

Health is the state of being well. Most people think health just means not being sick. This is true, but it's not the full story. Picture a triangle with three equal sides to see health in a new way.

Each side of the triangle stands for a different part of health: physical, mental, and social. People who care for all three parts can gain in overall strength, balance, and happiness.

- **Physical** health is about how the body works. It involves the foods you choose, the exercise you get, rest, sleep, and hygiene (keeping clean). This is the kind of health most people think of first.
- **Mental** health is about how the mind works, thinks, and feels. It involves ideas, emotions, and reactions, all of which affect your views on life.
- **Social** health is about getting along with people—family, friends, and others. It is about care, respect, and support—both giving and getting.

1. How does the triangle figure help explain this idea?

_____

_____

2. Which term best relates to social health?
   ○ A. hygiene   ○ B. emotions   ○ C. cooperation   ○ D. fitness

🌀 BrainTeaser 🌀

Find the extra word in each sentence and cross it out.

1. Some people are able to speak three or languages.

2. A mule is a cross word between a horse and a donkey.

3. The sign warns hikers to watch tower out for rattlesnakes.

4. I always sit in a window seat belt if there is one available.

5. The Lowry Park Zoo is a very popular with family visitors.

6. The class will put on a play about lumberjack Paul Bunyan and.

Reading & Math Practice, Grade 4 © 2014 Scholastic Inc.

Number Place

Write 3 decimals that belong between.

2 < _____ < 3

12 < _____ < 13

5.5 < _____ < 6

9 > _____ > 8

80 > _____ > 79

3.2 > _____ > 3.1

FAST Math

Find the difference in simplest form.

$6 \frac{2}{6}$
$- \ 3 \frac{1}{6}$
_____

$4 \frac{4}{5}$
$- \ 1 \frac{3}{5}$
_____

$7 \frac{5}{8}$
$- \ 4 \frac{4}{8}$
_____

$7 \frac{7}{9}$
$- \ 5 \frac{4}{9}$
_____

$8 \frac{6}{7}$
$- \ 7 \frac{4}{7}$
_____

$12 \frac{7}{8}$
$- \ 7 \frac{5}{8}$
_____

$8 \frac{4}{5}$
$- \ 7 \frac{1}{5}$
_____

$9 \frac{2}{3}$
$- \ 7$
_____

Think Tank

A tennis court is a rectangle 78 feet long and 27 feet wide. What is the area of a tennis court?

_____

Show your work in the tank.

Data Place

The chart shows five holidays in Mexico.

Use the data and your number sense to place and label each holiday on the timeline.

Constitution Day	February 5
Benito Juarez Birthday	March 19
Cinco de Mayo	May 5
Independence Day	September 16
Revolution Day	November 19

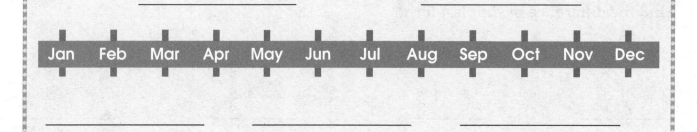

Jan Feb Mar Apr May Jun Jul Aug Sep Oct Nov Dec

Puzzler

Each problem is shown in mostly letters.
Above each problem are the rest of the numbers it needs.

Figure out the number for each letter to make the problems work.

1, 2, 4, 6, 8		2, 3, 6	
N B Q × 6 ‾‾‾‾‾‾ B, N W Q	□ □ □ × □ ‾‾‾‾‾‾ □,□ □ □	C C C K‾)‾T‾T‾T	□ □ □ □‾)‾□‾□‾□

186

Reading & Math Practice, Grade 4 © 2014 Scholastic Inc.

WORD of the Day

Use the word below in a sentence about using a hand lens.

magnify: (v.) *to make something look larger than it really is*

_____

_____

Sentence Mender

Rewrite the sentence to make it correct.

Pleas leaf your sootcase hear why'll you by you're ticket.

_____

Cursive Quote

Copy the quotation in cursive writing.

Be careful what you say because it can hurt more than a knife.

—Indonesian proverb

- -

- -

- -

How can words hurt as much as a knife wound can? Write your answer in cursive on another sheet of paper.

Analogy of the Day

Complete the analogy.

Leg is to **limb** as _____ is to **music**.

○ A. flute   ○ B. arm   ○ C. drama   ○ D. jazz

Explain how the analogy works: _____

_____

Ready, Set, READ!

Read the story. Then answer the questions.

Inside a Square Foot

Henry's task was to write an observer's journal. The teacher gave the assignment. Henry guessed he'd finish in a flash until she added, "Good observers take their time. They look slowly and carefully, close and hard. Give yourself time to get acquainted with the space inside your frame. You can't see everything in one glance."

The class trudged out to the hillside. Henry chose a shady spot and sat on his knees. He set his empty frame on the grass and started scanning the square inside it. At first, he saw only a solid green patch. Then he stooped down extremely close.

That's when his square foot revealed texture and life. Blades of grass stood at every height and angle. They were yellow, brown, and a dozen shades of green. Ants marched through as if on a mission. Henry noticed twigs, a rusty nail, and a striped feather. A ladybug crawled onto the feather, adding a splash of bright color. Henry grabbed his clipboard and pencil . . .

1. What did Henry think of the assignment at first? _____

_____

2. How did his attitude change? _____

_____

☺ BrainTeaser ☺

Use the clues to complete each word that includes *cap*.

1. Flowing garment   C A P ____

2. Summary   ____ ____ C A P

3. Adventure   C A P ____ ____

4. Get away   ____ ____ C A P ____

5. Cover for a car's wheel   ____ ____ ____ C A P

6. Words below a picture   C A P ____ ____ ____ ____

7. City where government is   C A P ____ ____ ____ ____

8. Ship commander   C A P ____ ____ ____ ____

Reading & Math Practice, Grade 4 © 2014 Scholastic Inc.

Number Place

Write 3 decimals that belong between.

$\frac{9}{10}$ > _____ > $\frac{5}{10}$

$\frac{2}{5}$ < _____ < $\frac{4}{5}$

12 < _____ < $12\frac{1}{2}$

$8\frac{1}{4}$ < _____ < $8\frac{3}{4}$

$5\frac{1}{5}$ < _____ < $5\frac{3}{5}$

$3\frac{1}{4}$ < _____ < $3\frac{1}{2}$

FAST Math

Find the product.

$\frac{1}{3}$ of 12 = _____

$\frac{1}{2}$ of 18 = _____

$\frac{1}{3}$ of 24 = _____

$\frac{1}{10}$ of 20 = _____

$\frac{1}{4}$ of 16 = _____

$\frac{1}{8}$ of 32 = _____

$\frac{1}{5}$ of 40 = _____

$\frac{1}{6}$ of 18 = _____

$\frac{1}{8}$ of 48 = _____

Think Tank

A book has 120 pages. One eighth of the pages have pictures. Two eighths have graphs. The rest of the book's pages have text only. What fraction of the book has neither pictures nor graphs?

_____

Show your work in the tank.

Data Place

The table shows scoring in the National Football League. The scoreboard shows the last time the Melons played the Pumpkins.

Touchdown	6 points
Touchdown With Extra Point	7 points
Field Goal	3 points
Safety	2 points

Use the clues to fill in the scoreboard.

Quarter	1	2	3	4	Final Score
Melons	3				
Pumpkins	2	3	6		

- The Melons scored a touchdown in the 2nd quarter.

- The Melons scored a touchdown with an extra point in the 3rd quarter.

- The Pumpkins scored a field goal in the fourth quarter.

- The Melons won the game by 4 points.

Puzzler

Use logic to figure out what a *nerp* is. Then solve.

EACH of these is a *nerp*.	□	◇	▱	▭
NONE of these is a *nerp*.	○	⬡	△	⚑

Circle all the *nerps*.

What is the rule for a *nerp*? _____

_____

WORD of the Day

Use the word below in a sentence about a sports stadium.

capacity: (n.) *the amount of space inside; volume; the greatest measure an object can hold*

_____

_____

Sentence Mender

Rewrite the sentence to make it correct.

We finish two hole water melons at the class picknick.

_____

Cursive Quote

Copy the quotation in cursive writing.

It's not what happens to you, but how you react to it that matters.
                                                        —Epictetus

- -

- -

- -

This saying is about 2,000 years old. Do you think it is true today?
Write your answer in cursive on another sheet of paper.

Analogy of the Day

Complete the analogy.

State is to **nation** as _____ is to **band**.

○ A. drummer   ○ B. capital   ○ C. song   ○ D. Virginia

Explain how the analogy works: _____

_____

📖 Ready, Set, READ!

Read the passage. Then answer the questions.

Supply and Demand

Economics is the science of buying and selling. It looks at how money affects us. Two big economic ideas are supply and demand.

Supply is how much of something is available. If you have 8 muffins to sell, your supply is 8. *Demand* is how much of something people want. If 10 people want muffins, the demand is 10. Supply and demand are related. They are usually discussed together. Prices can help explain the connection.

If the demand is high, the price usually goes up. If the demand goes down, the price usually goes down. Take sneakers. Popular new sneakers can cost a lot. This is because the demand for them is high. Older sneakers are usually a lot cheaper. This is because fewer people want them. When the demand is down, so is the price.

1. What is economics?
   ○ A. supply and demand
   ○ B. study of buying and selling
   ○ C. study of shopping
   ○ D. science of selling sneakers

2. What might cause prices to rise?
   ○ A. decrease in interest
   ○ B. increase in shopping malls
   ○ C. decrease in demand
   ○ D. increase in demand

🌀 BrainTeaser 🌀

Write the missing word for each three-word expression.

1. flesh and _____

2. knock on _____

3. bite your _____

4. rule of _____

5. rise and _____

6. _____ of cake

7. _____ and then

8. _____ the bucket

9. _____ from scratch

10. _____ your horses

Reading & Math Practice, Grade 4 © 2014 Scholastic Inc.

Number Place

Write the number that is *0.1* more.

2.2 _____   3.5 _____   7.8 _____

4.9 _____   6.61 _____   9.72 _____

Write the number that is *0.01* more.

3.23 _____   2.39 _____   9.06 _____

8.7 _____   54.09 _____   40 _____

FAST Math

Write each as an improper fraction.

$2\frac{2}{3}$ _____ $3\frac{1}{8}$ _____ $6\frac{1}{5}$ _____ $4\frac{3}{4}$ _____

$1\frac{7}{8}$ _____ $2\frac{5}{6}$ _____ $3\frac{4}{5}$ _____ $10\frac{1}{2}$ _____

Think Tank

Mori rode his bike $5\frac{3}{4}$ miles on Saturday and $4\frac{1}{4}$ miles on Sunday. Sam rode for $5\frac{1}{4}$ miles on each of those days. Who rode farther?

_____

By how much?

_____

Show your work in the tank.

Data Place

Use two dot cubes. Toss them 50 times. Make an X for each sum in the line plot below. Be sure you have 50 Xs in all.

What interesting things do you see in the data?

_____

_____

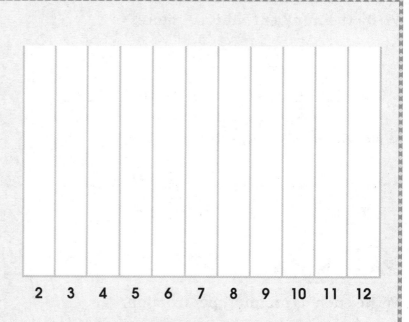

| 2 | 3 | 4 | 5 | 6 | 7 | 8 | 9 | 10 | 11 | 12 |

Puzzler

Solve each division problem. Then color.

RED if the remainder is even.

YELLOW if the remainder is odd.

BLUE if there is no remainder.

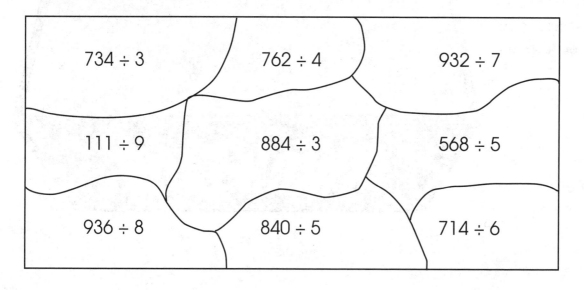

734 ÷ 3	762 ÷ 4	932 ÷ 7
111 ÷ 9	884 ÷ 3	568 ÷ 5
936 ÷ 8	840 ÷ 5	714 ÷ 6

WORD of the Day

Use the word below in a sentence about a roaring noise.

deafening: (adj.) *stunningly loud; earsplitting; booming*

_____

_____

Sentence Mender

Rewrite the sentence to make it correct.

Lake huron is the forth deepist of the five Great lake's.

_____

Cursive Quote

Copy the quotation in cursive writing.

I hear and I forget. I see and I remember. I do and I understand.

—Chinese proverb

- -

- -

- -

- -

Pretend you are the "I" in this proverb. Does it fit you? Write your answer in cursive on another sheet of paper.

Analogy of the Day

Complete the analogy.

Lens is to **camera** as _____ is to **computer**.

○ A. film   ○ B. desk   ○ C. monitor   ○ D. library

Explain how the analogy works: _____

_____

📖 Ready, Set, READ!

Read the passage. Then answer the questions.

An Enchanting Imp

The impish Puck has caused trouble for centuries. In older times, people believed in fairies and spirits, both good and evil. It was easy to blame them when things were confusing or went wrong.

William Shakespeare made Puck the key trouble-maker in his comedy *A Midsummer Night's Dream.* "I am that merry wanderer of the night," Puck says. He's a charming but annoying spirit. He plays tricks for fun. He makes fools of the humans to amuse the fairies.

This 500-year-old play is like a goofy sit-com. It takes place at night in an enchanted forest. Puck causes a string of mishaps and mix-ups. He makes a love potion but gives it to the wrong people! Actors rehearse a play to put on at a wedding. Puck finds their acting so bad that he turns one of them into a donkey! This makes their play even worse!

But in a comedy, things get sorted out by the end. Puck untangles all the messes, and everyone lives happily ever after.

1. Why were people long ago so willing to believe in fairies and spirits?

_____

_____

_____

_____

_____

_____

2. Which is the opposite of *comedy*?
   - ○ A. humor
   - ○ B. fiction
   - ○ C. tragedy
   - ○ D. poetry

🌀 BrainTeaser 🌀

How long a word link can you make? Link words by starting a new word with the *last* letter of the word before. This word link uses colors:

   yellow → white → eggshell → lavender

Continue the link of American places started below.

Think of towns, cities, islands, lakes, rivers, national parks, or states.

Idaho → Oklahoma → Albany → _____

_____

_____

_____

Reading & Math Practice, Grade 4 © 2014 Scholastic Inc.

Number Place

Write each money amount as a fraction or mixed number.

$4.27 _____   five dollars and twenty-five cents _____

$34.85 _____   eighteen dollars and seven cents _____

$.49 _____ $15.05 _____

FAST Math

Write each as a mixed number.

$\dfrac{8}{3}$ _____ $\dfrac{9}{8}$ _____ $\dfrac{11}{5}$ _____ $\dfrac{6}{5}$ _____

$\dfrac{17}{8}$ _____ $\dfrac{25}{6}$ _____ $\dfrac{24}{5}$ _____ $\dfrac{12}{10}$ _____

Think Tank

There are 24 students in Suki's class. One-half gets a ride to school. One-half of those comes by bus. How many students come by bus?

_____

Show your work in the tank.

Data Place

Ashley's Awful Foods is an awful place to eat. Check out today's lunch menu. Does it make you hungry?

Use the menu to answer the questions.

Dirt and Onion	
Sandwich.	$4.75
Pebble Pancakes	$3.95
Acorn Omelet	$3.25
Rubber Band Burger . . .	$4.20
All Drinks	$1.00

1. Dave orders pancakes and 1 drink. He pays with $10. What will his change be? _____

2. Omar orders the most expensive and least expensive foods. He has $10. Can he also buy a drink? _____ Explain. _____ _____

3. You have $15. You order 3 drinks. Can you order 3 burgers? _____ Explain. _____

4. Ella spent $5.95, including a tip of $1. She ordered a main course and a drink. What main course did she order? _____

Puzzler

A number cube has the numbers 1, 2, 3, 4, 5, and 6 on its faces. Here are two views of the same number cube. Answer the questions below.

What number is opposite the 2? _____

What number is opposite the 3? _____

What number is opposite the 6? _____

View 1   View 2

Reading & Math Practice, Grade 4 © 2014 Scholastic Inc.

WORD of the Day

Use the word below in a sentence about a doctor who is an expert in a certain branch of medicine.

specialize: (v.) *to make a special study of something or follow a certain branch of work*

_____

_____

Sentence Mender

Rewrite the sentence to make it correct.

The, axolotl or mexican walking fish, we now as a salamandar.

_____

Cursive Quote

Copy the quotation in cursive writing.

It does not matter how slow you go so long as you do not stop.
                                        —Confucius

_____

_____

_____

Explain in your own words what Confucius means. Write your answer in cursive on another sheet of paper.

Analogy of the Day

Complete the analogy.

Smart is to **brilliant** as _____ is to **beautiful**.

○ A. charming   ○ B. slow   ○ C. pretty   ○ D. sharp

Explain how the analogy works: _____

_____

📖 Ready, Set, READ!

Read the passage. Then answer the questions.

Three Branches of Government

The U.S. Constitution gives the rules of how our country is set up. It says that our government in Washington, D.C., will have three branches, or parts. The branches are equal. But each has a different job. Each branch has a different leader. Each works in a different place. Each branch has ways to affect the other two.

The chart can help explain the jobs.

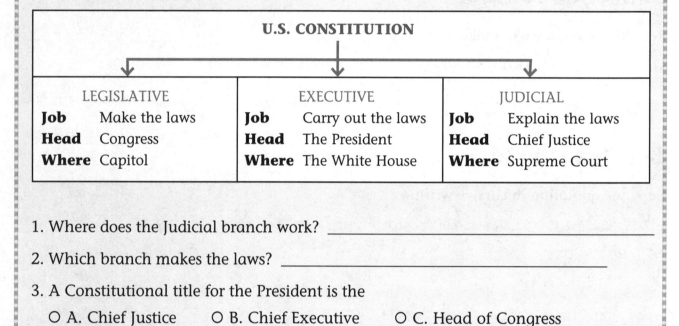

U.S. CONSTITUTION

LEGISLATIVE	EXECUTIVE	JUDICIAL
Job Make the laws	**Job** Carry out the laws	**Job** Explain the laws
Head Congress	**Head** The President	**Head** Chief Justice
Where Capitol	**Where** The White House	**Where** Supreme Court

1. Where does the Judicial branch work? _____

2. Which branch makes the laws? _____

3. A Constitutional title for the President is the

   ○ A. Chief Justice   ○ B. Chief Executive   ○ C. Head of Congress

🌀 BrainTeaser 🌀

What do lazy dogs do for fun and exercise?

Solve each clue. Then copy each letter into its numbered box to find the answer to the riddle.

• Decode the words

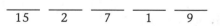
    8   5   13   11

• Small run-down hut

    15   2   7   1   9

• Scuff your knee

    4   12   14   3   6   10

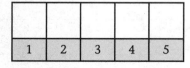

1	2	3	4	5

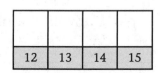

6	7	8	9	10	11

12	13	14	15

Number Place

Compare. Write **<**, **=**, or **>**.

0.5 _____ $\dfrac{1}{5}$ 0.2 _____ $\dfrac{1}{2}$ 0.7 _____ $\dfrac{3}{4}$

0.65 _____ $\dfrac{65}{100}$ $\dfrac{1}{2}$ _____ 0.2 $\dfrac{1}{6}$ _____ 0.1

$\dfrac{1}{4}$ _____ 0.4 $\dfrac{3}{4}$ _____ 0.8 $\dfrac{9}{10}$ _____ 0.9

FAST Math

Solve.

$\dfrac{1}{2}$ of 400 = _____ $\dfrac{1}{4}$ of 400 = _____ $\dfrac{1}{8}$ of 800 = _____

$\dfrac{1}{3}$ of 600 = _____ $\dfrac{1}{2}$ of 700 = _____ $\dfrac{1}{6}$ of 300 = _____

$\dfrac{1}{2}$ of $1{,}000$ = _____ $\dfrac{1}{2}$ of $5{,}000$ = _____ $\dfrac{1}{10}$ of $1{,}000$ = _____

Think Tank

There are 32 students in Carl's class. One-eighth of them send 10 or more texts a day. How many text at least 10 times a day?

_____

Show your work in the tank.

Data Place

The table shows miles between some cities in the state of Washington.

- Follow *across* a row for one city.
- Follow *down* a column for another.
- The number where they meet is how many miles apart they are.

Use the data in the table to answer the questions.

	Colville	Olympia	Wenatchee	Yakima
Seattle	350	60	148	141
Spokane	71	319	169	201
Tacoma	362	28	160	153

1. Which city is farthest from Seattle? _____

2. Which two cities are 319 miles apart? _____

_____

3. Which city is nearly as far from Spokane as it is from Tacoma?

_____

Puzzler

Follow the directions.

- Draw a ★ in each pentagon.
- Write a Q in each quadrilateral.
- Write an H in each hexagon.
- Draw an octopus in each octagon.

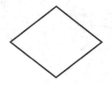 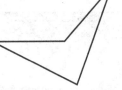

    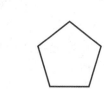

WORD of the Day

Use the word below in a sentence about taking something apart to see how it works.

mechanism: (n.) *a system of working parts in a machine*

_____

_____

Sentence Mender

Rewrite the sentence to make it correct.

He like her iced tee with alot of shugar or honie.

_____

Cursive Quote

Copy the quotation in cursive writing.

Patience: You get the chicken by hatching the egg, not by smashing it.
—Arnold H. Glasow

_____

_____

_____

What makes it so hard to be patient? Write your answer in cursive on another sheet of paper.

Analogy of the Day

Complete the analogy.

Steeple is to **church** as _____ is to **cake**.

○ A. sweet   ○ B. candle   ○ C. steep   ○ D. layer

Explain how the analogy works: _____

_____

📖 Ready, Set, READ!

Read the story. Then answer the questions.

I began hiking around the lake one misty October dawn. The bears and mountain lions were out seeking food. Signs posted at the trailhead warned people to hike in groups and not to bring pets along. They also advised making plenty of noise. So I hugged the lake shore and avoided any trail leading away from it into the thicker woods. I whistled as I walked.

I admit it, I was nervous. I kept my eyes peeled for anything moving that wasn't me. I walked for about ten minutes when I saw them: big fresh paw prints. I stopped dead in my tracks and examined them. These were nothing like the tracks house pets make. One big kitty had recently been here!

I was in no mood to startle a mountain lion or bump into a bear. I did an about-face that would suit a general. Then I sprinted to the safety of my car.

1. Why did the narrator whistle? _____

_____

2. What does it mean to "hug" the lake shore? _____

_____

3. Which would make the best title for this passage?

○ A. Hiking a Trail   ○ C. A Misty Dawn

○ B. Big Kitty   ○ D. A Quick Turn-Around

🌀 BrainTeaser 🌀

Homophones are words that sound the same but have different spellings and meanings. **Write the correct word in each sentence.**

1. That belt is too big for his _____.   **waist** *or* **waste**

2. Please _____ out your wet swim suit.   **ring** *or* **wring**

3. We dropped an _____ into the lake.   **ore** *or* **oar**

4. That bad cough left me a little _____.   **hoarse** *or* **horse**

5. Old paints used to be made with _____.   **lead** *or* **led**

6. Adult lions have such thick _____!   **mains** *or* **manes**

7. Today the dentist saw nine _____.   **patience** *or* **patients**

Reading & Math Practice, Grade 4 © 2014 Scholastic Inc.

Number Place

Compare. Write **<**, **=**, or **>**.

2.5 _____ $2\frac{1}{4}$ 1.25 _____ $1\frac{1}{4}$ 9.6 _____ $9\frac{1}{2}$

3.4 _____ $3\frac{3}{4}$ $8\frac{1}{2}$ _____ 8.2   3.7 _____ $3\frac{3}{4}$

3.9 _____ $3\frac{9}{10}$ $2\frac{1}{4}$ _____ 2.14   6.8 _____ $6\frac{3}{4}$

FAST Math

Find the answer. Watch the signs!

$$\begin{array}{r} 527 \\ \times\ \ \ \ 6 \\ \hline \end{array}$$ $4\overline{)981}$ $$\begin{array}{r} 68{,}507 \\ -\ 7{,}819 \\ \hline \end{array}$$ $$\begin{array}{r} \$35.06 \\ +\ \$27.85 \\ \hline \end{array}$$

$$\begin{array}{r} 3.4 \\ +\ \ 0.8 \\ \hline \end{array}$$ $$\begin{array}{r} 6.0 \\ -\ \ 0.7 \\ \hline \end{array}$$ $$\begin{array}{r} \$4.61 \\ -\ \ \$.88 \\ \hline \end{array}$$ $6\overline{)624}$

Think Tank

Which of the angles in the tank is an acute angle? Write its letter name.

_____

How did you know?

_____

_____

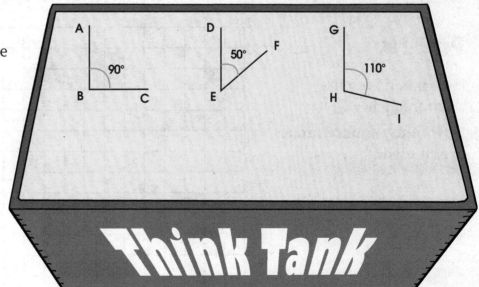

Data Place

The table shows stock market prices for three companies on one day. The decimals show prices in dollars.

Use the table to answer the questions below.

Company	Opening Price	High Price	Low Price	Closing Price
Dataworx	1.50	1.75	1.25	1.60
Healthco	8.15	8.80	8.15	8.75
Gametime	25.25	28.20	24.75	25.25

1. Which stock closed $.10 higher than it opened? _____

2. Which stock's high price was $.65 more than its opening price?

_____

3. Which stock's low price was the same as its opening price?

_____

4. Which stock had a difference of $3.45 between its lowest and highest price?

_____

Puzzler

Each box represents 1 square inch.

How many square inches are shaded?

_____

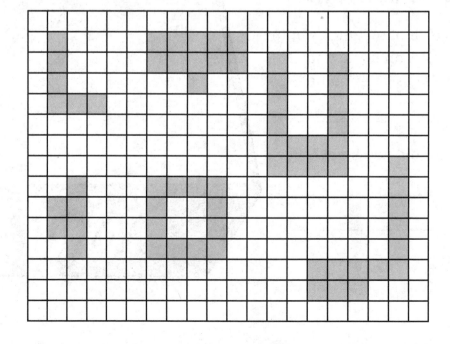

Reading & Math Practice, Grade 4 © 2014 Scholastic Inc.

WORD of the Day

Use the word below in a sentence about a call for help.

urgent: (adj.) *very important; needing serious action now*

_____

_____

Sentence Mender

Rewrite the sentence to make it correct.

Sorry son but You ain't the one who get to deside.

_____

Cursive Quote

Copy the quotation in cursive writing.

Even if happiness forgets you a little bit, never completely forget about it.

—Jacques Prévert

_____

_____

_____

How do you feel about Prévert's advice? Write your answer in cursive on another sheet of paper.

Analogy of the Day

Complete the analogy.

Thirsty is to **drink** as _____ is to **doze**.

○ A. tired   ○ B. hungry   ○ C. bed   ○ D. eat

Explain how the analogy works: _____

_____

Ready, Set, READ!

Read the passage. Then answer the questions.

A Noisy Dish?

"I'll have the bubble and squeak, please."

You don't hear people order that very often, do you? But in Great Britain, people do it all the time. Bubble and squeak is a common dish there. It is a classic comfort food made with leftover vegetables.

The main part of the dish is mashed potato. It is the glue that holds together everything else. The leftover vegetables may be carrots, Brussels sprouts, turnips, rutabagas, cabbage, leeks, spinach, beans, or onions. Bubble and squeak is a tasty way to get kids to eat their veggies. Add meat or fried eggs and you have a hearty lunch.

You might wonder about the dish's odd name. Some foods are named for the way they look, feel, smell, or taste. Examples include black-eyed peas, animal crackers, sloppy joes, or sauerkraut. Bubble and squeak is named for the *sounds* the potatoes make as they cook. First they bubble as they boil. Then they squeak as they fry. Eat up!

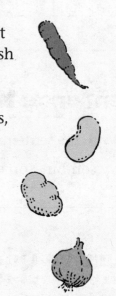

1. Where is bubble and squeak a popular dish? _____

_____

2. How did the dish get its name? _____

_____

ᕳ BrainTeaser ᕲ

Complete the category chart. The letters above each column
tell the first letter for each word.

	F	E	L	T
Foods				
Nations				
Movies				
Mammals				

Reading & Math Practice, Grade 4 © 2014 Scholastic Inc.

Number Place

Read the clues to figure out the number.

- I am a 4-digit decimal between 10 and 20.
- My tenths digit is twice my tens digit.
- The sum of my tenths and ones digits equals my hundredths digit.
- The sum of all my digits is 11.

What number am I? _____

FAST Math

Multiply. Circle the pair of products that have a sum of 5,100.

$$\begin{array}{r} 33 \\ \times\ 22 \\ \hline \end{array} \qquad \begin{array}{r} 23 \\ \times\ 11 \\ \hline \end{array} \qquad \begin{array}{r} 42 \\ \times\ 12 \\ \hline \end{array} \qquad \begin{array}{r} 48 \\ \times\ 99 \\ \hline \end{array}$$

$$\begin{array}{r} 64 \\ \times\ 39 \\ \hline \end{array} \qquad \begin{array}{r} 75 \\ \times\ 29 \\ \hline \end{array} \qquad \begin{array}{r} 62 \\ \times\ 42 \\ \hline \end{array} \qquad \begin{array}{r} 44 \\ \times\ 83 \\ \hline \end{array}$$

Think Tank

I am a quadrilateral. All my sides are the same length. But none of my angles are right angles. Draw me in the tank. What am I called?

_____

Show your thinking in the tank.

Data Place

The chart shows how Shakir exercises for an hour each day.

Show the data in the circle graph.

Outline, shade, and label each section with the exercise it stands for.

Write the number of minutes.

Exercise	Parts of an Hour
Sit-ups	$\frac{1}{12}$
Stretches	$\frac{1}{6}$
Treadmill	$\frac{8}{12}$
Weights	$\frac{1}{12}$

Exercises in One Hour

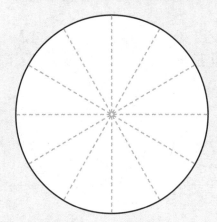

Puzzler

Half a bat appears on one side of a line of symmetry.

Shade in the rest of the bat.

Keep it symmetrical.

Answer Key

Reading 1
Word of the Day: Check the sentence for accurate usage of the term.
Sentence Mender: Our three puppies are Moe, Curly, and Larry. Note: the series comma before *and* is optional.
Cursive Quote: Check handwriting for accuracy and legibility. Check that the answer is reasonable.
Analogy of the Day: D; (object-location analogy) Check that the answer is reasonable.
Ready, Set, Read! 1. The balls of fluff were the two mutts.
2. Sample answer: I think they decided to adopt both puppies.
Brainteaser: Possible answer: limp, lime, line, fine

Math 1
Number Place: (Left to right) 302; 3,255; 7,287; 2,203; 2,761; 9,219; 223; 2,279; 2,196; 734; 5,305; 5,040
Fast Math: (Left to right) 11; 15; 15; 12; 15; 11; 16; 17; <u>18</u>
Think Tank: Ming
Data Place: 1. 24 **2.** 151 **3.** swimsuit
Puzzler: The picture is an inline skate.

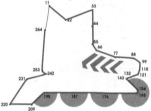

Reading 2
Word of the Day: Check the sentence for accurate usage of the term.
Sentence Mender: Can you name all fifty states of the United States?
Cursive Quote: Check handwriting for accuracy and legibility. Check that the answer is reasonable.
Analogy of the Day: B; (synonyms analogy) Check that the answer is reasonable.
Ready, Set, Read! 1. They do whatever work is needed on a farm, like picking fruit. **2.** Trey means that the taste is so amazing, his mouth will be delighted.
Brainteaser: 1. shoes **2.** shook **3.** shore **4.** should **5.** shower **6.** shovels

Math 2
Number Place: (Top to bottom) tens; hundreds; ten-thousands; thousands; ten-thousands; thousands; ten-thousands; hundreds; tens; hundred-thousands
Fast Math: (Left to right) 10; 7; 9; 9; 13; 8; 6; 8; 10
Think Tank: $10.95
Data Place: 1. 48 **2.** 8 **3.** altos and tenors **4.** sopranos
Puzzler:

6	7	2
1	5	9
8	3	4

Reading 3
Word of the Day: Check the sentence for accurate usage of the term.
Sentence Mender: No, I did not eat the last piece of candy.
Cursive Quote: Check handwriting for accuracy and legibility. Check that the answer is reasonable.
Analogy of the Day: C; (cause-and-effect analogy) Check that the answer is reasonable.
Ready, Set, Read! 1. B **2.** The merchant was ashamed that the child asked a question that was impossible for him to answer.
Brainteaser: 1. high **2.** comic **3.** going **4.** erase **5.** label **6.** razor **7.** dried **8.** yearly **9.** typist

Math 3
Number Place: 3,015; 29,437; 643,000; 82,311
Fast Math: <u>65</u>; 58; 96; 470; 790; 834
Think Tank: 5¢
Data Place: 1. Ridge **2.** Ridge and Old Mine **3.** Waterfall
Puzzler: 1. 800 **2.** 560 **3.** 132 = 1 hundred, 3 tens, 1 two **4.** 150 = 1 hundred, 4 tens, 5 twos

Reading 4
Word of the Day: Check the sentence for accurate usage of the term.
Sentence Mender: Bruno, who walks my dog, also waters the plants.
Cursive Quote: Check handwriting for accuracy and legibility. Check that the answer is reasonable.
Analogy of the Day: A; (antonyms analogy) Check that the answer is reasonable.
Ready, Set, Read! 1. The party is to celebrate Dad's new job. **2.** Potluck means that the guests must bring a food (in this case, a dessert) to share and nobody knows what may turn up.
Brainteaser: 1. sore **2.** lost **3.** rage **4.** lift **5.** crate **6.** alter/later **7.** sloop/loops/spool **8.** steer/reset

Math 4
Number Place: four thousand three hundred nineteen; forty-four thousand one hundred fifty-nine; twenty-seven thousand eight; sixty thousand six; three hundred nine thousand two hundred fifty-four
Fast Math: (Left to right) 7,426; 947; 619; 8,214; 5,963; 1,074; 8,214 + 619 = 8,833
Think Tank: Ben
Data Place: 1. 70 **2.** beaver **3.** 10 **4.** bear
Puzzler: 1. 17 **2.** 15 **3.** 5 **4.** 64

Reading 5
Word of the Day: Check the sentence for accurate usage of the term.
Sentence Mender: Tomorrow we will be visiting a bakery.
Cursive Quote: Check handwriting for accuracy and legibility. Check that the answer is reasonable.
Analogy of the Day: D; (class-example analogy) Check that the answer is reasonable.
Ready, Set, Read! 1. B **2.** Lion saw his own reflection in the pool.
Brainteaser: 1. Don't open your eyes yet. **2.** Would you like a second helping? **3.** Tomorrow is the first day of June. **4.** Could you bring the salad to the table?

Reading & Math Practice, Grade 4 © 2014 Scholastic Inc.

Math 5

Number Place:

Millions	Hundred-Thousands	Ten-Thousands	Thousands	Hundreds	Tens	Ones
3	0	5	2	8	0	4

Fast Math: 10,198; 43,181; 32,036
Think Tank: 15 eggs
Data Place: 1. 1 ticket = 10 students **2.** comedy **3.** 30 **4.** 170
Puzzler:

6	5	8	7
8	7	5	6
7	8	6	5
5	6	7	8

Reading 6

Word of the Day: Check the sentence for accurate usage of the term.
Sentence Mender: I'm reading the book Lizard Music by Daniel Pinkwater.
Cursive Quote: Check handwriting for accuracy and legibility. Check that the answer is reasonable.
Analogy of the Day: B; (antonyms analogy) Check that the answer is reasonable.
Ready, Set, Read! 1. D **2.** C
Brainteaser: Sample answers: **1.** clank **2.** crackles **3.** swoosh **4.** splat **5.** clatter

Math 6

Number Place:

Hundreds	or	Tens	or	Ones
3		30		300
6		60		600
18		180		1,800
27		270		2,700

Fast Math: (Top to bottom) 238,000; 510,000; 577,000; 104,000; 29,000; 935,000
Think Tank: $3.96
Data Place:

T-Shirt	Sizes			Total
	S	M	L	
Short Sleeve	27	35	42	**104**
Long Sleeve	36	**18**	21	75
V-Neck	49	9	31	89
Turtleneck	37	22	**27**	86
Sports Jersey	**9**	5	12	26

Puzzler:

Reading 7

Word of the Day: Check the sentence for accurate usage of the term.
Sentence Mender: Turn up the heat because it is too cold in here.
Cursive Quote: Check handwriting for accuracy and legibility. Check that the answer is reasonable.
Analogy of the Day: B; (part-whole analogy) Check that the answer is reasonable.
Ready, Set, Read! 1. They have the same number of lines and the same rhyme scheme. They also begin with the same words. **2.** They differ in how Isabella's family members reacted to her caterpillar. **3.** Her great-grandmother liked it the most.
Brainteaser: 1. words **2.** gold **3.** basket **4.** policy **5.** leap **6.** perfect **7.** worm **8.** tricks

Math 7

Number Place: 10; 100; 1,000; 10,000; 100,000
Fast Math: (Left to right) 8,807; 93,363; 71,362; 493,581; 9,361; 691,858
Think Tank: 22
Data Place:

Sandwich	Tally	Number
Peanut Butter	THL III	8
Grilled Cheese	THL THL THL I	16
Tuna	THL THL THL III	18
Hamburger	THL THL II	12

Puzzler: 15,359; 3,815; 536

Reading 8

Word of the Day: Check the sentence for accurate usage of the term.
Sentence Mender: The older children can make their own lunches.
Cursive Quote: Check handwriting for accuracy and legibility. Check that the answer is reasonable.
Analogy of the Day: D; (object-location analogy) Check that the answer is reasonable.
Ready, Set, Read! 1. Meaning 4. **2.** Sample sentence: The lantern sent out a beam of light into the cave.
Brainteaser: 1. bag tag **2.** mouse house **3.** book nook **4.** stamp champ **5.** strange change **6.** worn horn

Math 8

Number Place: (Top to bottom) 59,000; 899,000; 999,000; 3,399; 55,799; 1,000,000
Fast Math: (Left to right) 29,808; 120,359; 86,405; 942,112; 469,361; 1,401,714
Think Tank: 20
Data Place: 1. trapezoid **2.** quadrilateral with exactly 1 pair of parallel sides **3.** Check that the answer is reasonable.
Puzzler: 10; by identifying and counting groups of same-size segments.

Reading & Math Practice, Grade 4 © 2014 Scholastic Inc.

Reading 9

Word of the Day: Check the sentence for accurate usage of the term.
Sentence Mender: Jason asked, "Can you help me find my keys?"
Cursive Quote: Check handwriting for accuracy and legibility. Check that the answer is reasonable.
Analogy of the Day: B; (degree of meaning or synonyms analogy) Check that the answer is reasonable.
Ready, Set, Read! 1. D **2.** Sample answer: Scott wanted to let someone know where he was and why he wouldn't be home that night.
Brainteaser: 1. witty kitty **2.** boulder holder **3.** kitten mitten **4.** stranger danger **5.** jelly belly **6.** lucky ducky

Math 9

Number Place: (Top to bottom) 50,000; 890,000; 990,000; 127,399; 664,799; 988,888
Fast Math: (Left to right) <u>414</u>; <u>21</u>; 453; 1,127; <u>112</u>; 5,271
Think Tank: 185
Data Place: 1. 41 **2.** soccer **3.** hockey
Puzzler: Check the solution.

Reading 10

Word of the Day: Check the sentence for accurate usage of the term.
Sentence Mender: The science teacher gives us short quizzes every day.
Cursive Quote: Check handwriting for accuracy and legibility. Check that the answer is reasonable.
Analogy of the Day: C; (degree of meaning or synonyms analogy) Check that the answer is reasonable.
Ready, Set, Read! 1. It's hard because the outside points are all different distances from the center. **2.** Sample answer: Those two states are not attached to the other 48.
Brainteaser: (Top to bottom) polka, twist, tango, ballet, bolero, reel; partner

Math 10

Number Place: (Left to right) <; >; <; <; <; =
Fast Math: (Left to right) 4,337; <u>181</u>; 363; 533; 1,472; 2,391
Think Tank: 218 mi
Data Place: 1. 30 **2.** 9 **3.** 4 **4.** 6 **5.** 18
Puzzler: Sample answer: 175 + 326 + 498 = 999

Reading 11

Word of the Day: Check the sentence for accurate usage of the term.
Sentence Mender: How many legs do spiders have?
Cursive Quote: Check handwriting for accuracy and legibility. Check that the answer is reasonable.
Analogy of the Day: A; (object-action analogy) Check that the answer is reasonable.
Ready, Set, Read! 1. C **2.** B
Brainteaser: 1. plain **2.** supporter **3.** first **4.** tremble **5.** concern **6.** childish

Math 11

Number Place: 1,409; 4,190; 14,009; 12,007; 12,707; 21,700; 508,850; 805,058; 850,058; 12,200,000; 21,000,000; 210,200,000
Fast Math: (Left to right) 6,158; <u>1,671</u>; 379; 3,297; 79; 5,297
Think Tank: 19,669
Data Place: 1. Nov. 22, 23, and 24 **2.** Nov. 11 and 12 **3.** 260 **4.** 6
Puzzler: 1. ◄ = 2, △ = 5 **2.** ✳ = 6, ☺ = 3

Reading 12

Word of the Day: Check the sentence for accurate usage of the term.
Sentence Mender: They took the bus to see their grandmother in Kansas.
Cursive Quote: Check handwriting for accuracy and legibility. Check that the answer is reasonable.
Analogy of the Day: A; (example-class analogy) Check that the answer is reasonable.
Ready, Set, Read! 1. She knew how much fun it was to get a card you didn't expect. **2.** Sample answer: They might feel lonely or tired, and they might miss their families.
Brainteaser:

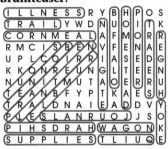

Math 12

Number Place:

Hundreds	or	Tens	or	Ones
4		40		400
16		160		1,600
90		900		9,000
240		2,400		24,000
4,100		41,000		410,000

Fast Math: (Left to right) 40,945; 7,341; 45,313; <u>63,377</u>; 1,115; <u>88,268</u>
Think Tank: 12; 38
Data Place: 1. Rangers **2.** Marlins **3.** Cardinals got 5 times as many votes as Tigers.
Puzzler:

24	47	71	86	14	37	22
101	59	7	105	96	11	26
12	23	89	9	98	72	66
49	5	116	37	20	36	55
81	35	56	87	78	122	27
60	75	123	45	80	44	70
8	138	35	21	17	43	117

Reading 13

Word of the Day: Check the sentence for accurate usage of the term.
Sentence Mender: Would you like butter or sour cream on your baked potato?
Cursive Quote: Check handwriting for accuracy and legibility. Check that the answer is reasonable.
Analogy of the Day: D; (object-description analogy) Check that the answer is reasonable.
Ready, Set, Read! 1. A **2.** D **3.** It probably got blown inside out.
Brainteaser: (Top to bottom) cloud, flute, hosts, kneel, pearl; fourth column: utter

Math 13
Number Place:

Number	Nearest 10	Nearest 100
617	620	600
1,862	1,860	1,900
4,345	4,350	4,300
89,083	89,080	89,100

Fast Math: Check that the estimates are reasonable; sample estimates: (Left to right) 10,000; 9,800; 90,000; 800,000; 11,000; 930,000
Think Tank: 1 quarter, 3 dimes, 1 nickel
Data Place: 1. Satellites **2.** Space Vacations **3.** Satellites **4.** Space Art **5.** Astronaut Training and Alien Life
Puzzler: Check the computations for accuracy.

Reading 14
Word of the Day: Check the sentence for accurate usage of the term.
Sentence Mender: We must start on time to finish the game by dark.
Cursive Quote: Check handwriting for accuracy and legibility. Check that the answer is reasonable.
Analogy of the Day: B; (object-user analogy) Check that the answer is reasonable.
Ready, Set, Read! 1. It is made only of snow. **2.** The spiral helps shape the dome; the angle of the blocks keeps the others in position. The weight of the blocks is also a factor.
Brainteaser: 1. not **2.** lets **3.** spoon **4.** bag **5.** money

Math 14
Number Place: (Top to bottom) 1,000; 10,000; 90,000; 400,000; 900; 300,000
Fast Math: (Left to right) 50,000; 5,500; 500,000; 25,000; 200,000; 770,000
Think Tank: 54 ft or 18 yd
Data Place: 1. $750.00 **2.** $136.04 **3.** bracelet, watch **4.** $184.99 **5.** ring and earrings
Puzzler: parallelogram

Reading 15
Word of the Day: Check the sentence for accurate usage of the term.
Sentence Mender: Oh, my goodness! We won the raffle!
Cursive Quote: Check handwriting for accuracy and legibility. Check that the answer is reasonable.
Analogy of the Day: A; (synonyms analogy) Check that the answer is reasonable.
Ready, Set, Read! 1. Valo is a dragon who can't breathe fire. **2.** She tells him that when he gets older, he'll be able to. **3.** B
Brainteaser: 1. flute **2.** harp **3.** drums **4.** trumpet **5.** bagpipes **6.** trombone **7.** organ **8.** recorder **9.** guitar **10.** tambourine

Math 15
Number Place: (Top to bottom) 900,000; 192,870; 810,000; 400,000; 922,000; 240,000
Fast Math: (Left to right) $11.67; $.09; $122.54; $863.52; $622.95; $253.67
Think Tank: 54 m
Data Place: Check the table and graph for accuracy.
Puzzler: 265 − 138 = 127; 119 + 526 = 645; 682 − 337 = 345; 416 + 187 = 603; 842 − 83 = 759

Reading 16
Word of the Day: Check the sentence for accurate usage of the term.
Sentence Mender: Keep all knives away from small children.
Cursive Quote: Check handwriting for accuracy and legibility. Check that the answer is reasonable.
Analogy of the Day: D; (part-whole analogy) Check that the answer is reasonable.
Ready, Set, Read! 1. D **2.** Submarine crews give up a lot of comforts to do their jobs.
Brainteaser: Sample answers:

	B	E	S	T
Names of Cities	Boston	El Paso	Seattle	Tampa
Map Words	bridge	east	south	trail
Forest Things	bear	elm tree	squirrel	thorn
Kitchen Things	banana	eggbeater	skillet	toaster

Math 16
Number Place: 2,000 + 300 + 80 + 2; 40,000 + 300 + 6; 200,000 + 20,000 + 5,000 + 900 + 60; 600,000 + 10
Fast Math: Estimates may vary; check for reasonableness; sample estimates: (Left to right) $110; $35; $1,200; $300; $600; $740
Think Tank: 3 quarters, 1 dime, 3 nickels
Data Place: Multiples of 3 only—3, 6, 9, 12, 18, 21, 24, 27, 33, 36, 39, 42, 48; multiples of 5 only—5, 10, 20, 25, 35, 40, 50; both—15, 30, 45
Puzzler: Drawings will vary; check that 4 colors are used and that the same colors do not touch.

Reading 17
Word of the Day: Check the sentence for accurate usage of the term.
Sentence Mender: "How do you say the word for homework in Spanish?" asked Betsy.
Cursive Quote: Check handwriting for accuracy and legibility. Check that the answer is reasonable.
Analogy of the Day: D; (member-group analogy) Check that the answer is reasonable.
Ready, Set, Read! 1. Sample answer: They all rhyme, they all have two lines; they all give a way to predict rain. **2.** Sample answer: The one about the drawers and door means it's humid, so rain is likely.
Brainteaser: 2. how/who **3.** saw/was **4.** won/now **5.** not/ton **6.** tub/but

Math 17
Number Place: 765,321; 123,567; 765,312; 765,321
Fast Math: (Left to right) 27; 30; 28; 40; 0; 36; 42; 3; 42
Think Tank: 80 ft
Data Place: 1. 41 km **2.** Go through Pea, 25 km **3.** Carrot and Lettuce
Puzzler: 880; 100; 36

Reading 18
Word of the Day: Check the sentence for accurate usage of the term.
Sentence Mender: Mom likes chocolate-covered cherries best of all candies.
Cursive Quote: Check handwriting for accuracy and legibility. Check that the answer is reasonable.
Analogy of the Day: B; (object-function analogy) Check that the answer is reasonable.
Ready, Set, Read! 1. Pigment is something in nature that contains color. **2.** D
Brainteaser: Check the word list for accuracy.

Math 18
Number Place: 27,222
Fast Math: (Left to right) 72; 45; 49; 56; 0; 63; 8; 81; 48
Think Tank: Iris, 55 lb; Ivan, 65 lb
Data Place: 1. 30 **2.** cats **3.** 4 times **4.** More kids have dogs than any other kind of pet.
Puzzler: 30; by identifying and counting different-size rectangles.

Reading 19
Word of the Day: Check the sentence for accurate usage of the term.
Sentence Mender: Do you think there will be a fire drill today?
Cursive Quote: Check handwriting for accuracy and legibility. Check that the answer is reasonable.
Analogy of the Day: C; (object-function analogy) Check that the answer is reasonable.
Ready, Set, Read! 1. Sample answer: He might have eaten up all their cornmeal; he may have frightened or harmed the people. **2.** A
Brainteaser: 1. window **2.** knock **3.** gang **4.** edge **5.** trust **6.** loyal **7.** plump **8.** health **9.** rooster

Math 19
Number Place:

Amount	Nearest $1	Nearest $10
$6.17	$6	$10
$28.62	$29	$30
$843.45	$843	$840

Fast Math:
Break-apart numbers may vary for the second row of problems.

$7 \times 8 = (\underline{5} \times 8) + (2 \times 8)$ $6 \times 7 = (5 \times 7) + (\underline{1} \times 7)$
  $= \underline{40} + 16$ $= 35 + \underline{7}$
  $= 56$ $= 42$

$6 \times 9 = (\underline{5} \times 9) + (\underline{1} \times 9)$ $7 \times 9 = (\underline{5} \times 9) + (\underline{2} \times 9)$
  $= \underline{45} + \underline{9}$ $= \underline{45} + \underline{18}$
  $= \underline{54}$ $= \underline{63}$

Think Tank: 12:40 P.M.
Data Place: 1. 62,400 **2.** 12,000 **3.** $180 **4.** loge **5.** field level and upper deck
Puzzler: The picture is a hat.

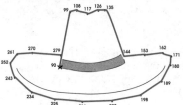

Reading 20
Word of the Day: Check the sentence for accurate usage of the term.
Sentence Mender: He watched in horror as a green snake crept toward the tent.
Cursive Quote: Check handwriting for accuracy and legibility. Check that the answer is reasonable.
Analogy of the Day: B; (object-description analogy) Check that the answer is reasonable.
Ready, Set, Read! 1. An ant farm is a protected area where ants can be observed as they work and eat. **2.** Sample answer: They changed their minds when they noticed how interesting it was to watch the ants.
Brainteaser: 1. prey **2.** press **3.** pretty **4.** prefer **5.** pretend **6.** predict **7.** pretzel

Math 20
Number Place:

Amount	Nearest $100	Nearest $1,000
$695.32	$700	$1,000
$1,230.55	$1,200	$1,000
$6,843.45	$6,800	$7,000

Fast Math: (Left to right) 120; 200; 240; 180; 350; 1,200; 3,000; 2,000; 2,100; 4,800; 1,800; 4,200
Think Tank: 0; any number multiplied by 0 is 0.
Data Place: 1. 80 lb; 40 lb **2.** 20 lb **3.** Stock is decreasing.
Puzzler:

Day	1	2	3	4	5	6	7	8	9	10
Pay	$.25	$.50	$1	$2	$4	$8	$16	$32	$64	$128

1. $100 **2.** $128

Reading 21
Word of the Day: Check the sentence for accurate usage of the term.
Sentence Mender: "Be home by four o'clock," said Dad.
Cursive Quote: Check handwriting for accuracy and legibility. Check that the answer is reasonable.
Analogy of the Day: A; (example-class analogy) Check that the answer is reasonable.
Ready, Set, Read! 1. He suggests that Idaho potatoes are enormous. **2.** Sample answer: It makes the potato seem bigger than the state itself!
Brainteaser: 1. baste **2.** claws **3.** grown **4.** overdue

Math 21
Number Place: $4.60; $27.34; $190.02; $2,015.50
Fast Math: (Left to right) 48,000; 24,000; 24,000; 28,000; 15,000; 72,000; 18,000; 56,000; 48,000
Think Tank: 4 ducks, 5 cows
Data Place: 1. 30 **2.** 9 **3.** 4 hours **4.** 3 **5.** 10
Puzzler: Sample answers:

	R	O	P	E	S
Number Words	Roman numeral	operation	plus	even	seven
Measurement Words	ruler	ounce	pound	equivalent	scale
Geometry Words	rectangle	octagon	polygon	equilateral	sphere

Reading 22
Word of the Day: Check the sentence for accurate usage of the term.
Sentence Mender: The book's silly title makes me laugh.
Cursive Quote: Check handwriting for accuracy and legibility. Check that the answer is reasonable.
Analogy of the Day: C; (antonyms analogy) Check that the answer is reasonable.
Ready, Set, Read! 1. D **2.** C
Brainteaser: (Top to bottom) pastel, frame, clay, felt, paint, crayon; tempera

Math 22
Number Place: (Left to right) <; >; <; >; <; >
Fast Math: (Left to right) 210; 240; 1,600; 3,200; 2,000; 7,200; 210; 5,400; 2,800
Think Tank: 16 times
Data Place: 1. 40-inch **2.** 32-inch **3.** 60-inch **4.** 400
Puzzler: Punxsutawney

Reading 23

Word of the Day: Check the sentence for accurate usage of the term.
Sentence Mender: "Strike three! You're out!" yelled the umpire.
Cursive Quote: Check handwriting for accuracy and legibility. Check that the answer is reasonable.
Analogy of the Day: D; (synonyms analogy) Check that the answer is reasonable.
Ready, Set, Read! 1. Sample answer: She needed to earn money for her family. **2.** She shares a small room in a boarding house near the mill.
Brainteaser: (Top to bottom) teach, those, titan, tower, truly; Henry

Math 23

Number Place: (Left to right) <; >; <; <; <; =
Fast Math: (Left to right) 3,500; 2,800; 16,000; 3,200; 20,000; 27,000; 1,800; 4,500; 24,000
Think Tank: 750
Data Place:

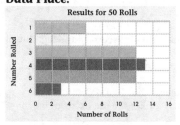

1. 3 and 5 **2.** 4
Puzzler: 1. 264 **2.** 104 **3.** 3,296 **4.** 2,484

Reading 24

Word of the Day: Check the sentence for accurate usage of the term.
Sentence Mender: I know all the words to all five verses of "This Land Is Your Land."
Cursive Quote: Check handwriting for accuracy and legibility. Check that the answer is reasonable.
Analogy of the Day: C; (example-class analogy) Check that the answer is reasonable.
Ready, Set, Read! 1. It is used two different times (in two different amounts) in the recipe. **2.** It means to push and press it with your hands.
Brainteaser: 1. occupied **2.** following **3.** blossom **4.** calm **5.** false

Math 24

Number Place: Sample answers: (Left to right) 2,145; 51,397; 7,075; 60,000; 89,002; 30,050
Fast Math: (Left to right) 280; 364; 76; 4,212; 1,896; 544; 2,766; 364; 5,257
Think Tank: 6 vans
Data Place: 1. $20.70 **2.** fish food, tank plant, ship **3.** 6 ships, $5.80
Puzzler: 1. ⅝, any fraction in eighths **2.** 1⅖, any mixed number equal to 1½

Reading 25

Word of the Day: Check the sentence for accurate usage of the term.
Sentence Mender: Arthur Wynne made the first crossword puzzle in 1913.
Cursive Quote: Check handwriting for accuracy and legibility. Check that the answer is reasonable.
Analogy of the Day: B; (object-function analogy) Check that the answer is reasonable.
Ready, Set, Read! 1. 9 feet tall **2.** Sample answer: It had the exact same life span as the grandfather; they got it when he was born, and it stopped working when he died.
Brainteaser: The nine-letter word is *hardcover*; other words will vary, but must include R and have at least three letters.

Math 25

Number Place: 30,003, 300,003; 10,001, 11,001; 200,007, 2,000,008; 1,006, 105
Fast Math: (Left to right) 180; 392; 1,588; 4,512; 4,896; 624; 1,866; 301; 3,355
Think Tank: bag of eyeballs and clown shoes
Data Place: Square 1: (1, 1), (1, 2), (2, 2), (2, 1); Square 2: (2, 2), (2, 4), (4, 4), (4, 2); Square 3: (3, 3), (3, 6), (6, 6), (6, 3); The numbers in the ordered pairs of the 3rd square are 3 times greater than the similar numbers in the 1st square.
Puzzler: Sample answers:

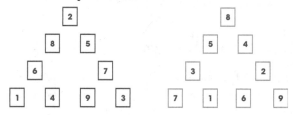

Reading 26

Word of the Day: Check the sentence for accurate usage of the term.
Sentence Mender: Ninth President William Henry Harrison served for less than thirty-one days.
Cursive Quote: Check handwriting for accuracy and legibility. Check that the answer is reasonable.
Analogy of the Day: D; (antonyms analogy) Check that the answer is reasonable.
Ready, Set, Read! 1. B **2.** He had only one hand.
Brainteaser: 1. lazy **2.** cozy **3.** zesty **4.** dozen **5.** breeze **6.** lizard

Math 26

Number Place: 101,005; 3,811, 4,981; 85,875, 100,500, 101,005; (Leftover numbers) 8,005, 9,005, 10,500, 20,530
Fast Math: (Left to right) $3.60; $2.80; $7.00; $13.38; $20.80; $17.10; $30.51; $2.01; $49.10
Think Tank: 73 points
Data Place:

Best Homework Spot	Tally	Number
Bed	IIII	4
Floor	卌 卌 卌 I	16
Table	卌 卌 卌 卌 卌 III	28

Puzzler:

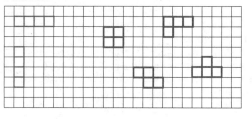

216

Reading 27

Word of the Day: Check the sentence for accurate usage of the term.
Sentence Mender: My uncle always sings a dumb song called "The Eggplant That Ate Chicago."
Cursive Quote: Check handwriting for accuracy and legibility. Check that the answer is reasonable.
Analogy of the Day: B; (antonyms analogy) Check that the answer is reasonable.
Ready, Set, Read! 1. D **2.** Sample answer: It teaches not to be greedy.
Brainteaser: 1. inning **2.** strike **3.** slugger **4.** bunt **5.** glove **6.** single **7.** steal **8.** triple **9.** mound **10.** fielder **11.** tag **12.** slide **13.** out **14.** catcher

Math 27

Number Place: 0.3; 0.6
Fast Math: (Left to right) 9; 9; 8; 10; 6; 0; 8; 10; 9
Think Tank: $15.30
Data Place: 1. Check the answer for accuracy. **2.** Check the answer for accuracy. **3.** 6 inches
Puzzler: 1. 5 × 447 **2.** 4 × 316

Reading 28

Word of the Day: Check the sentence for accurate usage of the term.
Sentence Mender: Jamille passed the test and got the highest score of anybody.
Cursive Quote: Check handwriting for accuracy and legibility. Check that the answer is reasonable.
Analogy of the Day: B; (part-whole analogy) Check that the answer is reasonable.
Ready, Set, Read! 1. D **2.** A
Brainteaser: rummy, aye, moo; Are you my mom?

Math 28

Number Place: 0.26; 0.47
Fast Math: (Left to right) 4; 8; 6; 8; 7; 0; 6; 7; 9
Think Tank: 2.5 g
Data Place:

In the Kennel	
Boxer	🐾🐾🐾🐾🐾🐾
Collie	🐾🐾🐾🐾🐾🐾🐾
Hound	🐾🐾🐾🐾🐾🐾🐾
Mutt	🐾🐾🐾🐾🐾🐾🐾🐾🐾🐾
Terrier	🐾🐾🐾🐾🐾
Key 🐾 = __4__ dogs	

Puzzler: addend; hexagon

Reading 29

Word of the Day: Check the sentence for accurate usage of the term.
Sentence Mender: "Where were you on Saturday, June 16, 2012, Dr. Miller?"
Cursive Quote: Check handwriting for accuracy and legibility. Check that the answer is reasonable.
Analogy of the Day: A; (object-description analogy) Check that the answer is reasonable.
Ready, Set, Read! 1. Molly **2.** The dog really can talk!
Brainteaser: 2. ring **3.** web **4.** basket **5.** oil **6.** pen

Math 29

Number Place: 7.4, 40.43; 7.14, 24.04; 4.01, 40.32
Fast Math: (Left to right) 4; 4; 4; 7; 5; 8; 6; 6; 7
Think Tank: 10
Data Place: 1. 56 **2.** Africa **3.** 8
Puzzler: 1. 99¢ **2.** 87¢ more

Reading 30

Word of the Day: Check the sentence for accurate usage of the term.
Sentence Mender: Can you believe that Alaska has a town called Y?
Cursive Quote: Check handwriting for accuracy and legibility. Check that the answer is reasonable.
Analogy of the Day: D; (user-object analogy) Check that the answer is reasonable.
Ready, Set, Read! 1. B **2.** A longer didj makes a lower tone; a shorter didj makes a higher tone.
Brainteaser: Sample answers: **1.** drain **2.** latch **3.** birdseed **4.** eraser **5.** timer **6.** soapdish **7.** folder **8.** mailbox **9.** playground **10.** pinecone

Math 30

Number Place: (Left to right) 0.3; 0.07; 0.62; 0.16; 0.9; 0.01
Fast Math: 270; 48, 480; 49, 490, 4,900; 70; 6, 60; 8, 80, 800
Think Tank: 4.4 m
Data Place: 1. Chrysler **2.** Hancock Place **3.** First Hawaiian Center
Puzzler: Sample answers: tulip (1, 3) (5, 0) (5, 2) (1, 1) (5, 1); oven (5, 4) (3, 5) (2, 4) (2, 0); grape (0, 0) (3, 1) (3, 2) (5, 1) (2, 4)

Reading 31

Word of the Day: Check the sentence for accurate usage of the term.
Sentence Mender: They shouldn't play their music so loud when kids are trying to sleep.
Cursive Quote: Check handwriting for accuracy and legibility. Check that the answer is reasonable.
Analogy of the Day: A; (cause-and-effect analogy) Check that the answer is reasonable.
Ready, Set, Read! 1. B **2.** Answers will vary; sample answer: It was during the day, so the room wasn't dark!
Brainteaser: Check the list of nouns.

Math 31

Number Place: (Left to right) >; <; <; >; <; =
Fast Math: 50; 70; 280; 280; 320; 540; 100, 400
Think Tank: 2.31 sec
Data Place: 1. 20 **2.** 50 **3.** 80 **4.** 7 **5.** 45; It is separated from the other scores.
Puzzler: 5,000 in the center, 1,000 opposite 4,000, and 2,000 opposite 3,000

Reading 32

Word of the Day: Check the sentence for accurate usage of the term.
Sentence Mender: Stephen Foster, the great American songwriter, was born on July 4, 1828.
Cursive Quote: Check handwriting for accuracy and legibility. Check that the answer is reasonable.
Analogy of the Day: B; (object-function analogy) Check that the answer is reasonable.
Ready, Set, Read! 1. The words in italics are Dr. Earle's own words. **2.** Sample answer: Without all that the ocean provides us, nothing on Earth would grow.
Brainteaser: Check the list of verbs.

Math 32

Number Place: 1.2, 1.5, 1.6, 1.9; 6.1, 6.4, 6.7, 6.8; 10.9, 10.6, 10.1, 0.4; 12.8, 12.7, 12.3, 11.9
Fast Math: Check that the estimates are reasonable; sample estimates: (Left to right) 5; 4; 60; 70; 40; 80; 7; 70; 100
Think Tank: 7,200 sec
Data Place:

	Number of Cousins	
Range	Tallies	Number
0–4	THL II	7
5–8	THL THL THL THL THL THL THL THL II	42
9–12	THL THL THL THL I	21
13–16	THL THL THL II	17
17 or more	THL IIII	9

1. 9–12 **2.** 9–12 **3.** Check the answer for accuracy.
Puzzler: Check that the design is symmetrical.

Reading 33

Word of the Day: Check the sentence for accurate usage of the term.
Sentence Mender: "May I please have your autograph, Prince William?"
Cursive Quote: Check handwriting for accuracy and legibility. Check that the answer is reasonable.
Analogy of the Day: A; (antonyms analogy) Check that the answer is reasonable.
Ready, Set, Read! 1. B **2.** Verse 1: all things that show their beauty in speed; verse 2: all things that show their beauty in slowness. **3.** It means powerful.
Brainteaser: Sample answer: Horrible Helen has hungry hamsters helping her hoist her helicopter.

Math 33

Number Place: (Left to right) >; <; >; >; <; =
Fast Math: Estimates may vary; sample estimates: (Left to right) 50; 50; 600; 60; 900; 400; 700; 400; 700
Think Tank: 1,140 ft
Data Place:

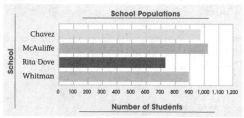

Check that the graph is reasonable; Rita Dove, Chavez, Whitman, McAuliffe
Puzzler:

Reading 34

Word of the Day: Check the sentence for accurate usage of the term.
Sentence Mender: Our summer garden in full bloom is as pretty as a picture.
Cursive Quote: Check handwriting for accuracy and legibility. Check that the answer is reasonable.
Analogy of the Day: C; (degree of meaning or synonyms analogy) Check that the answer is reasonable.
Ready, Set, Read! 1. B **2.** A
Brainteaser: Sample answer: cork, conk, honk, hunk

Math 34

Number Place: 1.02, 1.05, 1.06, 1.92; 4.47, 6.14, 6.43, 6.73; 10.91, 10.06, 10.01, 9.99; 12.37, 12.23, 11.23, 10.16
Fast Math: (Left to right) 24; 24; 16; 14; 38; 21; 51; 22; 32
Think Tank: 12 cups
Data Place: 1. Chicago **2.** Houston, Los Angeles **3.** New York **4.** about 2 million
Puzzler:

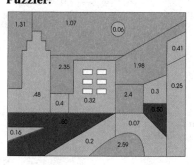

Reading 35

Word of the Day: Check the sentence for accurate usage of the term.
Sentence Mender: Let's put some beans, cucumbers, cheese, and beets in the salad. Note: the series comma before *and* is optional.
Cursive Quote: Check handwriting for accuracy and legibility. Check that the answer is reasonable.
Analogy of the Day: B; (part-whole analogy) Check that the answer is reasonable.
Ready, Set, Read! 1. Sample answers: 1) Tornadoes are violent storms that twist; 2) the Grand Canyon was once filled with water; 3) Death Valley is below sea level and is in California. **2.** D
Brainteaser: (Top to bottom) 3, 7, 6, 2, 1, 4, 5

Math 35

Number Place:

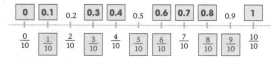

Fast Math: (Left to right) 75 R6; 53; 44; 33 R4; 18 R2; 14 R1; 20 R4; 139 R1
Think Tank: 1¾ or 1½ hours
Data Place: 1. 26 **2.** ¾ **3.** ¾ **4.** 22, ²²/₂₆ (or ¹¹/₁₃)
Puzzler: 22 geese, 14 goats

Reading & Math Practice, Grade 4 © 2014 Scholastic Inc.

Reading 36

Word of the Day: Check the sentence for accurate usage of the term.

Sentence Mender: Whose winter coat has lost its hood?

Cursive Quote: Check handwriting for accuracy and legibility. Check that the answer is reasonable.

Analogy of the Day: C; (part-whole analogy) Check that the answer is reasonable.

Ready, Set, Read! 1. Sample answer: It can help them be less embarrassed about having no hair. **2.** The writer includes Anthony's very own words.

Brainteaser: finds, sash, hip; fish and ships

Math 36

Number Place:

Tens	Ones	.	Tenths	Hundredths
1	4	.	5	9
2	0	.	0	6

Fast Math: (Left to right) 180; 208; 1,450; 85 R6; 170 R4; 652 R2

Think Tank: 375 minutes, or 6 hours 15 minutes

Data Place: 1. Apr. 17, 18, 19, and 20 **2.** Apr. 15 and 16 **3.** Apr. 24 and 8 **4.** Apr. 9 and 12

Puzzler: 1. 3:22, 4:14 **2.** 11:55, 12:30

Reading 37

Word of the Day: Check the sentence for accurate usage of the term.

Sentence Mender: Which one of these new songs did you like the least?

Cursive Quote: Check handwriting for accuracy and legibility. Check that the answer is reasonable.

Analogy of the Day: D; (doer-action analogy) Check that the answer is reasonable.

Ready, Set, Read! 1. C **2.** Sample answer: Perhaps that would be a better, safer, easier, more respected job.

Brainteaser: Check the word list for accuracy.

Math 37

Number Place: (Left to right) >; >; >; <; <; <

Fast Math: (Left to right) 800; 2,008; 1,453 R1; 859 R2; 204 R4; 544 R4

Think Tank: 70 sit-ups

Data Place: 1. 560 **2.** The Mangoes **3.** Popped Corn **4.** Louder Still

Puzzler: Pictures will vary; check that 64 and 35 boxes, respectively, have been shaded.

Reading 38

Word of the Day: Check the sentence for accurate usage of the term.

Sentence Mender: It's totally impossible to keep your eyes open when you sneeze.

Cursive Quote: Check handwriting for accuracy and legibility. Check that the answer is reasonable.

Analogy of the Day: C; (object-description analogy) Check that the answer is reasonable.

Ready, Set, Read! 1. This was a way to show mutual trust. **2.** The author tells where it came from in history and gives a modern example.

Brainteaser: (Top to bottom) at, ate, team, meant, mental, mantels, ailments

Math 38

Number Place: 0.09, 0.35, 0.42; 0.2, 0.43, 0.63; 0.04, 0.38, 0.4; 0.06, 0.57, 0.75

Fast Math: $\frac{1}{4}$; $\frac{2}{3}$; $\frac{5}{6}$; $\frac{2}{5}$

Think Tank: 3.2 mi

Data Place: 1. Rose to Lilac **2.** Lilac to Crocus **3.** 9:56 A.M. **4.** 12:19 P.M.

Puzzler: Drawings will vary; check that 4 colors are used and that the same colors do not touch.

Reading 39

Word of the Day: Check the sentence for accurate usage of the term.

Sentence Mender: An ostrich's eye is bigger than its brain!

Cursive Quote: Check handwriting for accuracy and legibility. Check that the answer is reasonable.

Analogy of the Day: D; (antonyms analogy) Check that the answer is reasonable.

Ready, Set, Read! 1. Jaguar had weapons and fire, which the humans did not. **2.** Sample answer: Jaguar showed kindness to the man, but the man repaid his kindness with cruelty. That made them enemies.

Brainteaser:

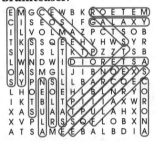

Math 39

Number Place: 8.05; 8.5; 3.75; 3.97

Fast Math: $2\frac{2}{3}$; $1\frac{1}{5}$; $3\frac{1}{2}$; $2\frac{1}{4}$

Think Tank: about $20

Data Place: 1. 20,000 **2.** 10,000 **3.** 115,000 **4.** It has mostly been increasing.

Puzzler: Accept any reasonable answers; sample answers: 3:00; 6:00; 3:40; 1:00

Reading 40

Word of the Day: Check the sentence for accurate usage of the term.

Sentence Mender: The world's heaviest onion weighed more than a man's head!

Cursive Quote: Check handwriting for accuracy and legibility. Check that the answer is reasonable.

Analogy of the Day: A; (example-class analogy) Check that the answer is reasonable.

Ready, Set, Read! 1. A prequel is a story that comes before the original story. **2.** They can keep readers interested by making the story unpredictable, and giving it lots of variety.

Brainteaser: 1. ten/net **2.** gel/leg **3.** den/end **4.** war/raw **5.** Sue/use **6.** Now/own

Reading & Math Practice, Grade 4 © 2014 Scholastic Inc.

Math 40

Number Place: 3.49, 3.35, 3.12; 8.63, 8.49, 8.2; 7.43, 7.4, 7.04; 20.75, 20.7, 20.07

Fast Math: (Left to right) $\frac{1}{5} + \frac{1}{5} + \frac{1}{5}$; $\frac{1}{7} + \frac{1}{7} + \frac{1}{7} + \frac{1}{7}$; $\frac{1}{8} + \frac{1}{8} + \frac{1}{8}$; $\frac{1}{9} + \frac{1}{9} + \frac{1}{9} + \frac{1}{9} + \frac{1}{9}$; $\frac{1}{8} + \frac{1}{8} + \frac{1}{8} + \frac{1}{8} + \frac{1}{8} + \frac{1}{8} + \frac{1}{8}$; $\frac{1}{11} + \frac{1}{11} + \frac{1}{11} + \frac{1}{11} + \frac{1}{11} + \frac{1}{11} + \frac{1}{11} + \frac{1}{11}$

Think Tank: 264

Data Place:

Vowel	Tally	Number
a	𝍸	5
e	𝍸	5
i	𝍸	5
o	𝍸	5
u	|	1
y	||	2

Puzzler:

Total Weight	Weights Used
975 grams	**750 kg + 225 g**
1,800 grams	**1 kg + 750 g + 50 g**
2,300 grams	**1 kg + ½ kg + 750 g + 50 g**

Reading 41

Word of the Day: Check the sentence for accurate usage of the term.

Sentence Mender: Each tiger has unique stripes, almost like people have fingerprints.

Cursive Quote: Check handwriting for accuracy and legibility. Check that the answer is reasonable.

Analogy of the Day: B; (object-user analogy) Check that the answer is reasonable.

Ready, Set, Read! 1. C **2.** Both are designs worn on the skin; but mehndi are temporary and are painted on.

Brainteaser: 1. ajar **2.** jazz **3.** eject **4.** major **5.** banjo **6.** enjoy **7.** object

Math 41

Number	Nearest tenth	Nearest hundredth
6.177	**6.2**	**6.18**
1.852	**1.9**	**1.85**
4.335	**4.3**	**4.33**

Fast Math: (Left to right) 3; 2; 4; 6; 2; 4; 3; 10; 1; 6; 9; 21

Think Tank: Fran's; 2¢ cheaper per pear

Data Place: Check that line plot matches the data in the tally table; sample summary: There were more cars than any other kind of vehicles, and there were the same number of trucks and buses.

Puzzler: 65¢; 70¢

Reading 42

Word of the Day: Check the sentence for accurate usage of the term.

Sentence Mender: Yesterday she was too sick to go to school, but today she is better.

Cursive Quote: Check handwriting for accuracy and legibility. Check that the answer is reasonable.

Analogy of the Day: C; (part-whole analogy) Check that the answer is reasonable.

Ready, Set, Read! 1. D **2.** The list explains the different customs for each of the five days of Diwali.

Brainteaser: Check the list of adjectives.

Math 42

Number Place: (Left to right) 0.4; 0.25; 1.5; 3.9; 2.75; 1.75; 7.25; 0.7; 5.8

Fast Math: (Left to right) $\frac{4}{8}$ or $\frac{1}{2}$; $\frac{4}{12}$ or $\frac{1}{3}$; $\frac{6}{7}$; $\frac{3}{10}$; $\frac{5}{9}$; $\frac{6}{11}$; $\frac{6}{6}$ or 1; $\frac{6}{5}$ or $1\frac{1}{5}$; $\frac{5}{8}$; $\frac{2}{10}$ or $\frac{1}{5}$

Think Tank: 58°F

Data Place: Multiples of 4 only—4, 8, 16, 20, 28, 32, 40, 44; multiples of 6 only—6, 18, 30, 42; both—12, 24, 36, 48

Puzzler:

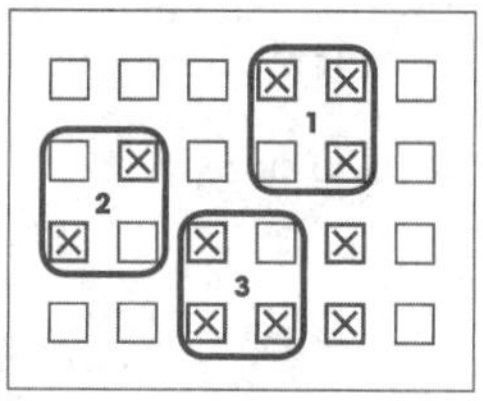

Reading 43

Word of the Day: Check the sentence for accurate usage of the term.

Sentence Mender: Yes, Jared practices his piano lesson for fifteen minutes a day.

Cursive Quote: Check handwriting for accuracy and legibility. Check that the answer is reasonable.

Analogy of the Day: B; (object-description analogy) Check that the answer is reasonable.

Ready, Set, Read! 1. D **2.** C

Brainteaser: (Top to bottom) 5, 7, 2, 3, 4, 1, 6

Math 43

Number Place: (Left to right) $\frac{35}{100}$ or $\frac{7}{20}$; $4\frac{6}{10}$ or $4\frac{3}{5}$; $3\frac{75}{100}$ or $3\frac{3}{4}$; $\frac{17}{100}$; $5\frac{97}{100}$; $4\frac{63}{100}$; $\frac{85}{100}$ or $\frac{17}{20}$; $60\frac{5}{10}$ or $60\frac{1}{2}$

Fast Math: (Left to right) 14; $6\frac{1}{5}$; $7\frac{2}{3}$; 9; $9\frac{4}{9}$; $7\frac{3}{4}$; $11\frac{4}{5}$; $5\frac{1}{4}$

Think Tank: 44 square units

Data Place: 1. 12 **2.** steak **3.** tuna **4.** $\frac{27}{60}$ or $\frac{9}{20}$ **5.** 24

Puzzler: 1. H **2.** E **3.** B **4.** J **5.** Z **6.** G **7.** L **8.** E

Reading 44

Word of the Day: Check the sentence for accurate usage of the term.

Sentence Mender: Her truly favorite athlete is soccer player David Beckham.

Cursive Quote: Check handwriting for accuracy and legibility. Check that the answer is reasonable.

Analogy of the Day: D; (synonyms analogy) Check that the answer is reasonable.

Ready, Set, Read! 1. The triangles equally represent the three parts of complete health. **2.** C

Brainteaser: 1. or **2.** word **3.** tower **4.** belt **5.** a **6.** and

Math 44

Number Place: Sample answers: (Left to right) 2.1, 2.2, 2.3; 8.5, 8.3, 8.1; 12.5, 12.6, 12.7; 79.9, 79.8, 79.7; 5.6, 5.7, 5.8; 3.17, 3.16, 3.15

Fast Math: (Left to right) $3\frac{1}{6}$; $3\frac{1}{5}$; $3\frac{1}{8}$; $2\frac{1}{3}$; $1\frac{2}{7}$; $5\frac{1}{4}$; $1\frac{3}{5}$; $2\frac{2}{3}$

Think Tank: 2,106 ft^2

Data Place:

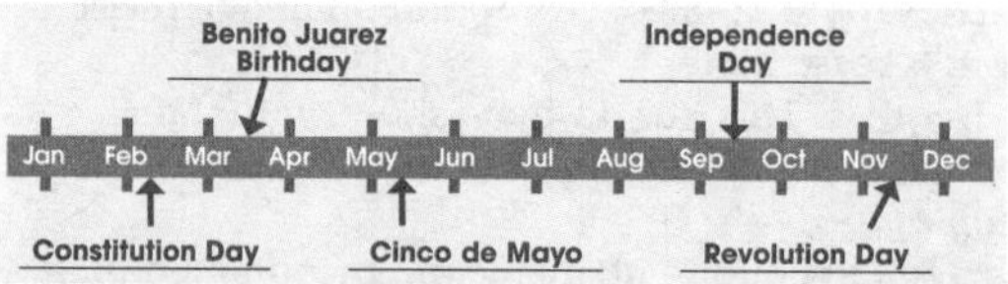

Puzzler: 6 × 214 = 1,284; 666 ÷ 2 = 333 (or 666 ÷ 3 = 222)

Reading & Math Practice, Grade 4 © 2014 Scholastic Inc.

Reading 45

Word of the Day: Check the sentence for accurate usage of the term.
Sentence Mender: Please leave your suitcase here while you buy your ticket.
Cursive Quote: Check handwriting for accuracy and legibility. Check that the answer is reasonable.
Analogy of the Day: D; (example-class analogy) Check that the answer is reasonable.
Ready, Set, Read! 1. Henry thought the assignment would be quick and easy. **2.** His attitude changed once he began to look closely and carefully at the space inside the frame.
Brainteaser: 1. cape **2.** recap **3.** caper **4.** escape **5.** hubcap **6.** caption **7.** capital **8.** captain

Math 45

Number Place: Sample answers: (Left to right) 0.8, 0.7, 0.6; 0.5, 0.6, 0.7; 12.2, 12.3, 12.4; 8.22, 8.23, 8.24; 5.3, 5.4, 5.5; 3.26, 3.27, 3.28
Fast Math: (Left to right) 4; 9; 8; 2; 4; 4; 8; 3; 6
Think Tank: ⅝
Data Place:

Quarter	1	2	3	4	Final Score
Melons	3	6	7	2	18
Pumpkins	2	3	6	3	14

Puzzler:

A *nerp* is a quadrilateral.

Reading 46

Word of the Day: Check the sentence for accurate usage of the term.
Sentence Mender: We finished two whole watermelons at the class picnic.
Cursive Quote: Check handwriting for accuracy and legibility. Check that the answer is reasonable.
Analogy of the Day: A; (part-whole analogy) Check that the answer is reasonable.
Ready, Set, Read! 1. B **2.** D
Brainteaser: 1. blood **2.** wood **3.** tongue **4.** thumb **5.** shine **6.** piece **7.** now **8.** kick **9.** start **10.** hold

Math 46

Number Place: (Left to right) 2.3; 3.6; 7.9; 5.0; 6.71; 9.82; 3.24; 2.4; 9.07; 8.71; 54.1; 40.01
Fast Math: (Left to right) ⅜; ²⅝; ³⅕; ¹¼; ¹⅝; ¹⅞; ¹⅖; 2½
Think Tank: Sam; by ½ mi
Data Place: Check the line plot and observations.
Puzzler:

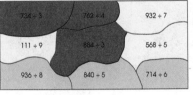

Reading 47

Word of the Day: Check the sentence for accurate usage of the term.
Sentence Mender: Lake Huron is the fourth deepest of the five Great Lakes.
Cursive Quote: Check handwriting for accuracy and legibility. Check that the answer is reasonable.
Analogy of the Day: C; (part-whole analogy) Check that the answer is reasonable.
Ready, Set, Read! 1. They didn't always understand how the world worked, so they blamed things on spirits and fairies instead. **2.** C
Brainteaser: Sample answer: Yellowstone, Endicott, Texas, Springfield, Delaware, Easton, Nevada . . .

Math 47

Number Place: (Left to right) 4²⁷⁄₁₀₀; 5²⁵⁄₁₀₀ or 5¼; 34⁸⁵⁄₁₀₀ or 34¹⁷⁄₂₀; 18⁷⁄₁₀₀; ⁴⁹⁄₁₀₀; 15⁵⁄₁₀₀ or 15¹⁄₂₀
Fast Math: (Left to right) 2⅔; 1⅛; 2⅕; 1⅕; 2⅛; 4⅙; 4⅘; 1²⁄₁₀ or 1⅕
Think Tank: 6
Data Place: 1. $5.05 **2.** yes; the foods = $8 **3.** no; 3 × $4.20 > $12 **4.** pebble pancakes
Puzzler: 5; 4; 1

Reading 48

Word of the Day: Check the sentence for accurate usage of the term.
Sentence Mender: We know the axolotl, or Mexican walking fish, as a salamander.
Cursive Quote: Check handwriting for accuracy and legibility. Check that the answer is reasonable.
Analogy of the Day: C; (degree of meaning or synonyms analogy) Check that the answer is reasonable.
Ready, Set, Read! 1. Supreme Court **2.** Legislative **3.** B
Brainteaser: read, shack, scrape; chase parked cars

Math 48

Number Place: (Left to right) >; <; <; =; >; >; <; <; =
Fast Math: (Left to right) 200; 100; 100; 200; 350; 50; 500; 2,500; 100
Think Tank: 4
Data Place: 1. Colville **2.** Spokane and Olympia **3.** Wenatchee
Puzzler:

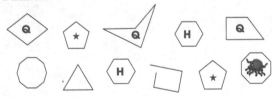

Reading 49

Word of the Day: Check the sentence for accurate usage of the term.
Sentence Mender: He likes his iced tea with a lot of sugar or honey.
Cursive Quote: Check handwriting for accuracy and legibility. Check that the answer is reasonable.
Analogy of the Day: B; (object-location analogy) Check that the answer is reasonable.
Ready, Set, Read! 1. The narrator was trying to make noise so any nearby wild animals wouldn't be surprised. **2.** Sample answer: It means to stay near to the water's edge. **3.** D
Brainteaser: 1. waist **2.** wring **3.** oar **4.** hoarse **5.** lead **6.** manes **7.** patients

Math 49

Number Place: (Left to right) >; =; >; <; >; <; =; >; >
Fast Math: (Left to right) 3,162; 245 R1; 60,688; $62.91; 4.2; 5.3; $3.73; 104
Think Tank: *DEF;* it is smaller than a right angle.
Data Place: 1. Dataworx **2.** Healthco
3. Healthco **4.** Gametime
Puzzler: 64

Reading 50

Word of the Day: Check the sentence for accurate usage of the term.
Sentence Mender: Sorry, son, but you aren't the one who gets to decide.
Cursive Quote: Check handwriting for accuracy and legibility. Check that the answer is reasonable.
Analogy of the Day: A; (cause-and-effect analogy) Check that the answer is reasonable.
Ready, Set, Read! 1. Great Britain **2.** It is named for the cooking sounds of the potatoes.
Brainteaser: Sample answers:

	F	E	L	T
Foods	French fries	eggs	lettuce	tuna
Nations	Fiji	Egypt	Laos	Tanzania
Movies	Finding Nemo	E.T.	Lady and the Tramp	Toy Story

Math 50

Number Place: 13.25
Fast Math: (Left to right) 726; 253; 504; 4,752; <u>2,496</u>; 2,175; <u>2,604</u>; 3,652
Think Tank: rhombus
Data Place:

Puzzler: Check that the drawing is symmetrical.

Reading & Math Practice, Grade 4 © 2014 Scholastic Inc.

You can use this page to work out your answers.

Reading & Math Practice, Grade 4 © 2014 Scholastic Inc.

You can use this page to work out your answers.